Book Synopsis

"God's Shifting Power" reveals the true realities that occur when shifting with God. Receive revelation and strategies on how to deal with the processes of shifting as you stay focus in transitioning with God. Also learn kingdom worship strategies and weapons that pull down religious and traditional strongholds related to praise and worship and the arts ministry within the church, exposes Satan's plans to displace the destiny of God's church and the younger generations, that shift us from emotional encounters to true transformation of self, our ministry, our region, and nation, while establishing the kingdom of God in the earth.

GOD'S SHIFTING POWER!
SHIFTTTTTTTTTTTT!

TaquettaBaker@Kingdomshifters.com

(Website) Kingdomshifters.com

Connect with Taquetta via Facebook or YouTube

Copyright 2014 – Kingdom Shifters Ministries

All rights reserved. This book is protected by the copyright laws of the United States of America. This book may not be reprinted for commercial gain or profit. The use of occasional page copying for personal or group study is permitted and encouraged. Permission will be granted upon request.

Taquetta's Bio

Taquetta Baker is the founder of Kingdom Shifters Ministries (KSM). She has authored fourteen books and two decree CD's. Taquetta has a Master's Degree in Community Counseling with an emphasis on Marriage, Children and Family Counseling, a Bachelor's Degree in Psychology and Associates Degree in Business Administration. In addition, Taquetta has a Therapon Belief Therapist Certification from Therapon Institute and has 22 years of professional and Christian Counseling experience.

Taquetta is also gifted at empowering and assisting people with launching ministries, businesses and books and provides mentoring, counseling and vision casting through Kingdom Shifters Kingdom Wellness Program.
Taquetta serves on the Board of Directors for New Day Community Ministries, Inc. of Muncie, IN. In October 2008, Taquetta graduated from the Eagles Dance Institute under Dr. Pamela Hardy and received her license in the area of liturgical dance. Before launching into her own ministry, Taquetta served at her previous church for 12 years. She was a prophet, pioneer and leader of Shekinah Expressions Dance Ministry, teacher, member of the presbytery board, and overseer of the Altar Workers Ministry. Taquetta receives mentoring and ministry covering from Bishop Jackie Green, Founder of JGM-

National PrayerLife Institute (Phoenix, AZ), and was ordained as an Apostle on June 7, 2014.

Taquetta flows through the wells of warfare and worship and mantles an apostolic mandate of judging and establishing God's kingdom in people, ministries, communities, and regions. Taquetta travels in foreign missions and throughout the United States. She has mentored and established dance, altar workers, deliverance, and prophetic ministries. Taquetta ministers in the areas of fine arts, all manners of prayer, fivefold ministry, deliverance, healing, miracles, atmospheric worship, and empowers and train people in their destiny and life's vision.

Connect with Taquetta and KSM at kingdomshifters.com or via Facebook. For more information regarding Bishop Jackie Green at Jgmenternational.org

Table of Contents

Remnant Arise & Conquer	1
Remnant Arising Decree	9
Dunamis Power of Shifting	11
Dunamis Power Decree	27
Types of Shifts	29
Kingdom Realities of Shifting	42
Releasing The Old When Shifting	47
Loss, Shock & Trauma In The Shift	51
The Process Of A Destiny Shift	57
Immovable Decree!	70
Unity in Shifting Atmospheres	72
Kingdom War Club Movement	91
The Shifting Power Of The Battering Rams	110
Weapons Of Song & The Tongue	115
The Sound Of The Glory Minstrel	130
The Glory Roar	145
Rend the Heavens	159

FORWARD

Shifting is a continuous process that impacts us personally, regionally, and nationally, while establishing the Kingdom of God in the earth. The Lord reveals different aspects of shifting as we began to unify and align with His ordained destiny individually and as a body of Christ. As we grow in a deeper relationship with the father we will encounter different types of shifts that will occur in our lives. These shifts are what help align us with what he has called us to be and do in every season that we go through.

The process of shifting is not easy but as yield ourselves, our gifts, our callings, our desires, and our wants we will see that the Lord is purifying our wells and positioning us to have a greater impact in our regions and spheres of influence so that we can establish the Kingdom of God all the more in the earth.

The author of "God's Shifting Power" has done an excellent job of depicting the realities of the shifting process, equipping us with tools to utilize during the shift, and understanding that the power of shifting atmospheres and regions is in us as we align with Him.

"God's Shifting Power" lets us see that shifting is about transformation and newness. It causes us to come out of our emotions and to focus on what the Lord is saying to us and what He is requiring from us. This book leads us in truly yielding our will for his and receiving the fullness of what he has for us.

As you read "God's Shifting Power" be open the shifting process and receiving a new perspective. Yield yourself to *the cleansing, delivering, healing, and equipping power that comes with the process and allow God to really take the lead and absorb his truth as he begins to expose his design, destiny, and heart for you.*

Blessings,

Amanda Barnhill Muncie, IN

Taquetta's Mentee & Administrator

Remnant Arise & Conquer

I hear the Lord saying that He is looking for a remnant who really desire to be used of Him to take over regions. He is looking for a remnant who are truly willing to sell out to Him, in gifting, in calling, in time, and with investing in the regional vision that He is releasing. God says He has already spoken to some of you, but you are looking for numbers or you are saying, "I cannot do that Lord." "That vision is too big." "That vision is impossible with just little ole me." God says He is not looking for numbers but a remnant. God says He is not looking for those who think they have already arrived. He says He is looking for the people who have room to be taught and who reverence Him with their lifestyle, such that they will seek Him for guidance of how to bring the vision to past and are willing to sacrifice self, sacrifice insecurities - sacrifice being in the in crowd, all while remaining constant in seeing the vision come to pass.

> *Matthew 18:18-20 - The Message Version*
> *Take this most seriously: A yes on earth is yes in heaven; a no on earth is no in heaven. What you say to one another is eternal. I mean this. When two of you get together on anything at all on earth and make a prayer of it, my Father in heaven goes into action (He shifts into action). And when two or three of you are together because of me, you can be sure that I'll be there (I'll shift into your midst).*

Two or three does not sound like much but God only need a faithful few - a remnant to bring forth His will and purpose in this hour.

> ***King James Version*** - *Verily I say unto you, whatsoever ye shall bind on earth shall be bound in heaven: and whatsoever ye shall loose on earth shall be loosed in heaven. Again I say unto you, that if two of you shall agree on earth as touching anything that they shall ask, it shall be done for them of my Father which is in heaven (God shifts into action). For where two or three are gathered together in my name, there am I in the midst of them (shifting into the midst of the agreement).*

Agree in the Greek is *Symphoneo* and means:
1. To be harmonious, i. e. (figuratively) to accord (be suitable, concur) or stipulate (by compact): — agree (together, with)
2. To agree with one in making a bargain, to make an agreement, to bargain

Dictionary.com defines *Harmonious* as:
1. Marked by agreement in feeling, attitude, or action
2. Forming a pleasingly consistent whole; congruous
3. Pleasant to the ear; tuneful; melodious

No matter how you say it, sing it, tune it up, dance it, play it, make melodies with it, the agreement produces a harmonious sound, a pleasant atmospheric melody that releases a reaction and visitation from God. God leaves heaven and come into your midst to complete an eternal work.

<u>Earth</u> in the Greek is *Ge* and means:
1. Soil; by extension a region, or the solid part or the whole of the terrene globe (including the occupants in each application)
2. Country, earth, earthly ground, land, world

We discern here that whatever you are agreeing about is not just being released in your life, but in the region, and even affects the earth globally. When the remnant agrees, we affect a sphere; we possess power to transform the land and even the world.

God is after specific regions so that He can establish His kingdom for the purposes of impacting the world. Will you accept your remnant assignment in your region?

> ***The Amplified Version*** - *Truly I tell you, whatever you forbid and declare to be improper and unlawful on earth must be what is already forbidden in heaven, and whatever you permit and declare proper and lawful on earth must be what is already permitted in heaven. Again I tell you, if two of you on earth agree (harmonize together, make a symphony together) about whatever [anything and everything] they may ask, it will come to pass and be done for them by My Father in heaven. For wherever two or three are gathered (drawn together as My followers) in (into) My name, there I AM in the midst of them.*

We are learning from these passages of scriptures that:
- What the remnant forbids and declares must be what is already illegal in heaven.
- There must be a harmonious agreement together as a symphony about whatever the remnant is forbidding and declaring in order to shift God into action.
- God then responds to the remnant being gathered together for His purpose and the full power of His name, which has the ability to produce everything we need and desire personally and in the region.

This is essential as often we desire miracles, signs, and wonders, and we desire to impact atmospheres and conquer regions, yet we lack unity in congregational worship, in ministries, among ministries, among the body of Christ in general. Therefore we lack the authority which is the key of agreement needed to take over regions and really see God's powers consistently manifest in the earth.

Reasons God is looking for a remnant is to:
- Combat the demonic sounds, movements, and frequencies that are being released from the demonic realm.
- The younger generations are really being drawn into the enemy's camp by the music and media industry. These demonic prophets and apostles are singing, dancing, and releasing sounds, movements, and frequencies that are altering the destiny of the younger generations.

It is essential that God's remnant shift into position to not only counterattack this unlawful and improper displacement, but release God's voice via song, movement, and melody; so that His word can override these demonic forces, and realign the generations into His ordained destiny. (Study Daniel 4:3, Psalms 78:4-8, Psalms 22:30-31, Psalms 45:17, Psalms 105:8, Acts 2:38-39)

Agreement and unity is what makes a remnant strong. They maybe small in number, but the power of oneness releases a gigantic God who is more powerful than all the people in the universe combined.

> *Isaiah 45:5-6 - New Living Translation - I am the LORD; there is no other God. I have equipped you for battle, though you don't even know me, so all the world from east to west will know there is no other God. I am the LORD, and there is no other.*
>
> *The Message Version - I am God, the only God there is. Besides me there are no real gods. I'm the one who armed you for this work, though you don't even know me, So that everyone, from east to west, will know that I have no god-rivals. I am God, the only God there is.*

Take a moment to recommit yourself as one of God's remnant:
- Repent for anyway you have not accepted your ordained calling as one of God's remnant set apart to establish His kingdom in your region.
- Release any fears, insecurities, vulnerabilities you have about being God's chosen remnant.
- Cleanse your gifts and calling from any sin or contamination that would prevent you from being a pure conduit for God to work through.
- Spend time asserting your authority in the region by interceding for the following prayer points:
    - Declare the remnant to come forth and for divine connections to occur to unify the remnant
    - Repent for sins in the land and for ways the demonic world has captivated the generations.
    - Call the arts ministry and generations from under the bewitchment of the demonic entertainment world and declare restoration and reconciliation with God.

Remnant Arising Scripture Declaration!
GOD IS WITH ME!

Romans 8:31-37 - *What, then, shall we say in response to these things? If God is for us, who can be against us? What then shall we say to [all] this? If God is for us, who [can be] against us? [Who can be our foe, if God is on our side?] He who did not withhold or spare [even] His own Son but gave Him up for us all, will He not also with Him freely and graciously give us all [other] things? Who shall bring any charge against God's elect [when it is] God Who justifies [that is, Who puts us in right relation to Himself? Who shall come forward and accuse or impeach those whom God has chosen? Will God, Who acquits us?]*

Who is there to condemn [us]? Will Christ Jesus (the Messiah), Who died, or rather Who was raised from the dead, Who is at the right hand of God actually pleading as He intercedes for us? Who shall ever separate us from Christ's love? Shall suffering and affliction and tribulation? Or calamity and distress? Or persecution or hunger or destitution or peril or sword? Even as it is written, For Thy sake we are put to death all the day long; we are regarded and counted as sheep for the slaughter. Yet amid all these things we are more than conquerors and gain a surpassing victory through Him Who loved us.

2Kings 6:16-17 - *Don't be afraid," the prophet answered. "Those who are with us are more than those who are with them. And Elisha prayed, and said, Lord, I pray thee, open his eyes, that he may see. And the Lord opened the eyes of the young man; and he saw: and, behold, the mountain was full of horses and chariots of fire round about Elisha.*

Isaiah 8:10 - *Devise your strategy, but it will be thwarted; propose your plan, but it will not stand, for God is with us.*

The Amplified Version - *Take counsel together [against Judah], but it shall come to nought; speak the word, but it will not stand, for God is with us [Immanuel]!*
Isaiah 41:10 - So do not fear, for I am with you; do not be dismayed, for I am your God. I will strengthen you and help you; I will uphold you with my righteous right hand.

Remnant Arising Decree!
GOD IS WITH ME!

God is with me! It is in His authority I stand. Fixed in His power, I establish my stance! I fear not because I am His Rising Remnant!

God is with me! His presence and word speak my truth! Their faces stare me down. Their intimidations wail in rage in effort to coward and cringe. But I just stand in God's sovereignty and await His revenge.

God is with me so I forgive quickly and pray grace for my foes. I truly want them on my side-God's side. My prayer is that they be made whole.

God is with me! I give no room to offense. I remain secure in knowing through God, I will prevail in the end.

God is with me! More of His kingdom is with me than with them. He is greater in me - a strength to which no one can contend.

God is with me! I rest my case in Him. At peace I stand immobile, immovable, locked in, even laughing at times at the fierce raging winds.

God is with me! The region I claim for His name. I claim my destiny and SHIFT into overtaking the region – establishing His holy name.

God is with me! No principality or power stands a chance. Demons will bow and flee! God's kingdom will take residence through the work of my hands.

God is with me! His word will not return void. My authority is in embracing His word and doing exactly what He says. His word will let all know that in my life, He is Lord!

**GOD IS WITH ME!
I AM A REMNANT ARISING!**

The Dunamis Power Of Shifting

SHIFTS are necessary to continually align us with destiny. God is always about growth and advancement. God's desire is for us to have life and that more abundantly that He promised. He is always improving and elevating us, His kingdom and the world.

- *Press Toward*

    Philippians 3:14 - *I press toward the mark for the prize of the high calling of God in Christ Jesus.*

    Expanded Version - *I keep trying to reach [pursuing; chasing] the goal and get the prize for which God called me to the life above [heavenward; upward] through [or in] Christ Jesus.*

- *Began a Good Work*

    Philippians 1:6 - *Being confident of this very thing, that he which hath begun a good work in you will perform it until the day of Jesus Christ:*

    Amplified Bible - *And I am convinced and sure of this very thing, that He Who began a good work in you will continue until the day of Jesus Christ [right up to the time of His return], developing [that good* *work] and perfecting and bringing it to full completion in you.*

- **Expected End**

    ***Jeremiah 29:11**- For I know the thoughts that I think toward you, saith the Lord, thoughts of peace, and not of evil, to give you an expected end.*

    ***English Standard Version** - For I know the plans I have for you, declares the LORD, plans for welfare and not for evil, to give you a future and a hope.*

- **When You Go**

    ***Matthew 10:7-8** - And as ye go, preach, saying, the kingdom of heaven is at hand. Heal the sick, cleanse the lepers, raise the dead, cast out devils: freely ye have received, freely give.*

    ***The Amplified Version** - And as you go, preach, saying, the kingdom of heaven is at hand! Cure the sick, raise the dead, cleanse the lepers, drive out demons. Freely (without pay) you have received, freely (without charge) give.*

Merriam Webster's Dictionary defines *Shift* as:
1. To exchange for or replace by another, change
2. To change the place, position, or direction of, to make a change in (place)

3. To change phonetically
    A. to change place or position
    B. To change direction
    C. To change gears
    D. To assume responsibility
    E. To resort to expedients
    F. To go through a change
    G. To change one's clothes
    H. To become changed phonetically

From the definition we receive some transparent revelation regarding Shifts:

- Shifts are inevitable
- Shifts will occur with are without our permission
- Shifts takes the course or path to which it originates from
- Everything we do or do not do has the ability to shift our lives, the lives of others, atmospheres, regions, etc.
- Everything we do or do not do determines the outcome of the shift
- Regardless to what we do or do not do we are causing an effect and a swaying and even a stance is taking place of what God we serve, who we belong too, and how we are impacted in a shift
- Shifts occur regardless of our willingness to flow with the shift. Even when we do not choose to flow with the shift that does not stop the shift from actually occurring

- Our choice in whether we embrace the shift or not determines where we align when the shifts happens
- Because we possess this innate power of shifting, God tells us all throughout the word to choose a side, and behooves us to never serve another other than Him - as when we do, our actions produce an effect and whether that be in our lives, the atmosphere, the lives of others, a shift takes place

Revelations 3:15-16 - *I know your works, that you are neither cold nor hot: I would you were cold or hot. So then because you are lukewarm, and neither cold nor hot, I will spew (vomit) you out of my mouth.*

<u>Works</u> in the Hebrew is *Ergon* or *Ergo* and means:
1. To work, toil (as an effort or occupation); by implication, an act, deed, doing, labour
2. Business, employment, that which any one is occupied that which one undertakes to do, enterprise
3. Undertaking any product whatever, anything accomplished by hand, art, industry, or mind, an act, deed, thing done
4. The idea of working is emphasized in opp. to that which is less than work

- When we are aligning with God, anything that is unhealthy will be exposed or pushed out as we shift
- Our work or lack of work produces a shift

- Being bias, lukewarm, toiling between two gods, two opinions or two stances produces a shift
- Being torn can affect how God deals with us which can also produce a shift

As kingdom people we should always be manifesting the light and glory of God in everything we do so that we shift His kingdom from heaven to earth. When we minister, witness, how we live and interact throughout the day, and even through our character and will, we should be shifting darkness to light so that God gets glory. We should also be planting Godly seeds where God's light can manifest and as someone else comes and waters what we plant, there is a shifting that takes place to solidify God's work in the earth.

When we shift heaven to earth we are executing a judgment from the Lord. This is the reason God tells is to be hot or cold, as the enemy has no legal right to judge us. He is not our creator. He is not our God. When we are lukewarm or serve the enemy, we put him in a position that really belongs to God. We also give the enemy rule to judge us and the Lord, and truly he does not have power to assert such authority. Who judges God?

> ***Ephesians 4:8-13 -*** *Wherefore he saith, when he ascended up on high, he led captivity captive, and gave gifts **(the gifts were a seed)** unto men. (Now that he ascended, what is it but that he also descended first into the lower parts of the earth? He that descended is the same also that ascended up far above all heavens, that he might fill all things).*

> *And he gave some, apostles; and some, prophets; and some, evangelists; and some, pastors and teachers; For the perfecting **(shifting)** of the saints, for the work **(shifting)** of the ministry, for the edifying **(shifting)** of the body of Christ: Till we all come in **(shift)** the unity of the faith, and of the knowledge of the Son of God, unto a perfect man, unto the measure of the stature of the fulness of Christ.*

Jesus shifted into hell conquered it, shifted to earth and filled every requirement needed to cause further shifting on earth by planting the seed of the gifts of men. And then Jesus shifted to heaven to establish the works He did in hell and on earth by taking His seat at the right hand of judgment with God. Jesus undid the shift that the enemy caused in the garden with Adam and Eve.

> ***Genesis 3:1-8*** *- Now the serpent was more subtle than any beast of the field which the Lord God had made. And he said unto the woman, Yea, hath God said, Ye shall not eat of every tree of the garden? And the woman said unto the serpent, we may eat of the fruit of the trees of the garden: But of the fruit of the tree which is in the midst of the garden, God hath said, Ye shall not eat of it, neither shall ye touch it, lest ye die.*
>
> *And the serpent said unto the woman, Ye shall not surely die: For God doth know that in the day ye eat thereof, then your eyes shall be opened, and ye shall be as gods, knowing good and evil. And when the*

*woman saw that the tree was good for food, and that it was pleasant to the eyes, and a tree to be desired to make one wise, she **took** of the fruit thereof, and did eat, and gave also unto her husband with her; and he did eat. And the eyes of them both were opened, and they knew that they were naked; and they sewed fig leaves together, and made themselves aprons.*

<u>The word *Took* is *Laqah* in the Hebrew and some of the definitions are as followed:</u>
1. means to seize, marry, to flash about (of lightning) (lightening denotes judgment)
2. send for, take away, carry away (you see the shift), capture

- When Adam and Eve ate from the tree of good and evil, they shifted the entire world and all of mankind out of the blessings and wholeness of the Lord into the hand of the enemy
- One demonic prophetic act of wanting to be like God shifted mankind into marriage with the enemy
- One demonic prophetic act of wanting to be like God shifted mankind from eternal life to death - from light into darkness

Jesus' coming to earth, restored our power over Satan and darkness.

Luke 10:17-20 - *And the seventy returned again with joy, saying, Lord, even the devils are subject unto us through thy name. And he said unto them,*

I beheld Satan as lightning fall from heaven. Behold, I give unto you power to tread on serpents and scorpions, and over all the power of the enemy: and nothing shall by any means hurt you.
Notwithstanding in this rejoice not, that the spirits are subject unto you; but rather rejoice, because your names are written in heaven.

In this passage of scripture, Jesus received a vision of regarding the seventy shifting the kingdom of God into the earth by casting out devils in His name. An exchange occurred as the kingdom of Satan was dismantled and the kingdom of God shifted into its place. Jesus even saw Satan fall as lightening. The light the disciples were dispelling was striking such that Satan's darkness was dispelled and plummeted him to the ground.

Jesus further expressed to the seventy that He had given them this power to trample on snakes and scorpions - trample on the devil without being harmed. Jesus is letting us know that it is essential to operate in the power of God to shift Satan and his king under our feet.

<u>*Power* is *Dunamis* in this passage of scripture and means:</u>
1. Power, mighty work, strength, miracle, might, virtue, mighty, ability
2. Inherent power, power residing in a thing by virtue of its nature, or which a person or thing exerts and puts forth
3. Power for performing miracles

4. Moral power and excellence of soul
5. The power and influence which belong to riches and wealth
6. Power and resources arising from numbers
7. Power consisting in or resting upon armies, forces

<u>Tread is *Pater* in the Greek and means:</u>
1. Path, to trample (literally or figuratively), tread (down, under foot)
2. To tread to trample, crush with the feet
3. To advance by setting foot upon, tread upon, trample under foot
4. To encounter successfully the greatest perils from the machinations (evil plots and purposes) and persecutions with which Satan would fain thwart
5. The preaching of the gospel,
6. To treat with insult and contempt: to desecrate the holy city by devastation and outrage

Dunamis power is what equips us to do mighty works for Jesus effectively and successfully, while treading on the wiles of the enemy. We are able to insult and crush wickedness and conquer with excellence, in our lives, ministries, regions and sphere of influence.

Jesus says we have power over serpents and scorpions. A serpent is *a sly, artfully malicious, cunning animal, person, idea, or scheme.*

<u>Scorpion</u> in the Greek is <u>Skerpo</u> and means:
1. Pierce, to sting or from its sting
2. The name of a little animal, somewhat resembling a lobster, which in warm regions lurk, esp. in stone walls; it has a poisonous sting in its tail

Wikipedia.com contends that *"stone walls are a kind of masonry construction which have been made for thousands of years. First they were constructed by farmers and primitive people by piling loose field stones in what is called a dry stone wall, then later with the use of mortar and plaster especially in the construction of city walls, castles, and other fortifications prior to and during the Middle Ages."*

Stone walls can be ancient walls, high places, and forts that have been built up against the divine government of Jesus. Stone walls can also be ideas, vain imaginations, rules, laws, and regulations that oppose or defy the truth of God.

If we are going to operate in God's shifting power, we must be filled with Jesus' power and have keen revelation of His Dunamis power working on the inside of us.

> **Acts 1:8** - *But ye shall receive power, after that the Holy Ghost is come upon you: and ye shall be witnesses unto me both in Jerusalem, and in all Judaea, and in Samaria, and unto the uttermost part of the earth.*

> **Romans 15:13** - *May the God of hope fill you with all joy and peace in believing, so that by the power of the Holy Spirit you may abound in hope.*
>
> **Luke 4:24** - *I am going to send you what my Father has promised; but stay in the city until you have been clothed with power from on high."*
>
> **Acts 2:1-2** - *And when the day of Pentecost was fully come, they were all with one accord in one place. And suddenly there came a sound from heaven as of a rushing mighty wind, and it filled all the house where they were sitting. And there appeared unto them cloven tongues like as of fire, and it sat upon each of them. And they were all filled with the Holy Ghost, and began to speak with other tongues, as the Spirit gave them utterance.*

In Acts 2, we have the 120 waiting on the outpouring of the power that Jesus had promised them. A rushing mighty wind came from heaven and through it cloven tongues of fire set upon each person. They were then filled with the Holy Ghost which is the Dunamis power of God.

<u>Cloven</u> in dictionary.com is defined as:
1. a past particle of cleave and cleave means to adhere closely, stick, cling, to remain faithful
2. Synonyms are open, rend, split, pierce, separate

When the Holy Spirit fills us with Dunamis power, it cleaves and clings to us. Though Dunamis possess the power to open, rend, split, pierce, and separate, it remains faithful – it never leaves us. In *Luke 4:24,* Jesus tells the disciples to wait in Jerusalem and expect to be endued with power from on high. That word "*endued*" means "*to be clothed or arrayed.*" Basically they were expecting to be clothed, like a garment or uniform, in the power of the Holy Spirit.

Many of us are clothed in the Holy Spirit but Jesus' Dunamis power is lying dormant upon and inside of us. Many of us have not really begun our path of using our power to tread on the enemy, or we use it when in crisis mode, or just enough to overcome some obstacles, but not enough to really establish the kingdom in and around us.

Operating in God's shifting power requires constant use of Dunamis power. You cannot overthrow Satan's kingdom without it. This is the reason Jesus had the disciples look for it. Jesus expects us to do greater works than Him and wants us to desire His Dunamis power.

> ***John 14:12*** - *Verily, verily, I say unto you, He that believeth on me, the works that I do shall he do also; and greater works than these shall he do; because I go unto my Father.*
>
> ***The Message Version*** - *Believe me: I am in my Father and my Father is in me. If you can't believe that, believe what you see – these works. The person who trusts me will not only do what I'm doing but even greater things, because I, on my way to the*

Father, am giving you the same work to do that I've been doing. You can count on it.

If we are filled with the Holy Spirit we can count on doing greater works if we just believe and pursue them.

Acts 2:17 - *And it shall come to pass in the last days, saith God, I will pour out of my Spirit upon all flesh. And your sons and your daughters shall prophesy, and your young men shall see visions, and your old men shall dream dreams.*

Amplified Version - *And it shall come to pass in the last days, God declares, that I will pour out of My Spirit upon all mankind, and your sons and your daughters shall prophesy [telling forth the divine counsels] and your young men shall see visions (divinely granted appearances), and your old men shall dream [divinely suggested] dreams.*

<u>Out</u> is <u>Cheo</u> <u>in the Greek and means:</u>
1. To pour, to pour forth; figuratively, to bestow
2. Gush (pour) out, run greedily (out), shed (abroad, forth), spill
3. Run out shed, run greedily, shed abroad, gush out, to pour out
4. Shed forth, metaph. to bestow or distribute largely

God is not stingy with the Holy Spirit. When God pours out His Spirit in an outpouring,
- He pours Himself out and runs greedily upon and into all who desires to partake of Him

- He wants the earth and His people to be prosperous in hearing His word and releasing His word
- He wants us to be equipped in being able to shift and produce heaven in the earth
- He is birthing and releasing His word so that it can produce power in the earth
- He is fulfilling prophecies and promises regarding His Spirit and regarding what He has spoken
- He is creating a hunger and expectation for even more of His Dunamis pour being poured out

Joel 3:18 - In that day the mountains will drip new wine, and the hills will flow with milk; all the ravines of Judah will run with water. A fountain will flow out of the LORD's house and will water the valley of acacias.

Isaiah 32:15 - Till the Spirit is poured on us from on high, and the desert becomes a fertile field, and the fertile field seems like a forest.

Job 7:38 - Whoever believes in me, as Scripture has said, rivers of living water will flow from within them."

Isaiah 44:3 - For I will pour water upon him that is thirsty, and floods upon the dry ground: I will pour my spirit upon thy seed, and my blessing upon thine offspring.

> **Ezekiel 34:26** - *I will make them and the places surrounding my hill a blessing. I will send down showers in season; there will be showers of blessing.*
>
> **Ezekiel 36:27** - *And I will put my Spirit in you and move you to follow my decrees and be careful to keep my laws.*

If you are not filled with the Holy Spirit, I encourage you to seek revelation and ask God to fill you as there is covenant blessings in the outpouring:

> **Micah 5:7** - *The remnant of Jacob will be in the midst of many peoples like dew from the LORD, like showers on the grass, which do not wait for anyone or depend on man.*
>
> **Isaiah 59:21** – *"As for me, this is my covenant with them," says the LORD. "My Spirit, who is on you, will not depart from you, and my words that I have put in your mouth will always be on your lips, on the lips of your children and on the lips of their descendants--from this time on and forever," says the LORD.*

If you are not treading in Dunamis power, I encourage you to begin your journey today. Start looking for people to pray for, seeking ways to snatch down Satan's kingdom, and even ask God to provide pathways for you to be use mightily for His glory. In addition, spend time seeking God for greater manifestations of His limitless power and to transform your character and nature in His likeness so that He can trust you with His power. This is important because though Jesus expressed to the disciples that He saw Satan fall like lightening, He also told them not to rejoice because of this, but because their names where in the book of heaven.

> ***Luke 10:17: 20*** - *Notwithstanding in this rejoice not, that the spirits are subject unto you; but rather rejoice, because your names are written in heaven.*

The more we have Jesus' humble spirit, the more we believe in greater works and the more we will be used to bring forth greater works. Jesus did works so that God could be glorified. It is important for us to have that same focus and fortitude.

> ***John 5:20*** - *For the Father loveth the Son, and sheweth him all things that himself doeth: and he will shew him greater works than these, that ye may marvel.*

Dunamis Power Decree

Decreeing you have a desire to be filled to the overflow with Jesus Dunamis power with the evidence of speaking in tongues which is God's voice and with all other ministry gifts and spirits fruits actively flowing in and through you.

Decreeing Jesus' Dunamis power is cleaving to you, clinging to you and that you are clothed in Dunamis power as an armored weapon.

Decreeing Dunamis power is your continual guide and source of spiritual and natural excellency and success.

Decreeing that you have revelation of Jesus's power in you and know that you can do all things through Jesus Christ who strengthens and empowers you.

Decreeing new dimensions of Jesus' Dunamis power is limitlessly activated in you even now, and you are pursuing the highest capacity available in allowing God to use you and get glory out of your life.

Decreeing you are being transformed in the image and likeness of Jesus such that people may marvel at God's awesomeness in you.

Decreeing that despite trials, tribulations, persecutions, rejections and life challenges, you are allowing Jesus' Dunamis power speak for you and defend the calling and destiny on your life.

Decreeing you are treading a continual journey of treading down Satan and His kingdom like lightening as Jesus' Dunamis power radiates from you with miracles and signs following.

Types of Shifts

God created the earth with His Spirit (shifting power) and shifting words:

> **Genesis 1:1-6** - *In the beginning God created the heaven and the earth. And the earth was without form, and void; and darkness was upon the face of the deep. And the Spirit of God moved upon the face of the waters. And God said, Let there be light: and there was light. And God saw the light, that it was good: and God divided the light from the darkness. And God called the light Day, and the darkness he called Night. And the evening and the morning were the first day. And God said, Let there be a firmament in the midst of the waters, and let it divide the waters from the waters.*

The word "*said*" is "*amar*" and means "to command, boast, answer, charge, declare, publish, avow, to say in one's heart, to think." When God spoke His desires, SHIFT, the world was so! WHEWWWWW! SHIFT!

Goliath scared the heck out of the Israelites through shifting words:

> **1Samuel 17:3-11**
> *And there went out a champion out of the camp of the Philistines, named Goliath, of Gath, whose height was six cubits and a span. And he had an helmet of brass upon his head, and he was armed with a coat of mail; and the weight of the coat was*

five thousand shekels of brass. And he had greaves of brass upon his legs, and a target of brass between his shoulders. And the staff of his spear was like a weaver's beam; and his spear's head weighed six hundred shekels of iron: and one bearing a shield went before him. And he stood and cried unto the armies of Israel, and said unto them, why are ye come out to set your battle in array?

Am not I a Philistine, and ye servants to Saul? Choose you a man for you, and let him come down to me. If he be able to fight with me, and to kill me, then will we be your servants: but if I prevail against him, and kill him, then shall ye be our servants, and serve us. And the Philistine said, I defy the armies of Israel this day; give me a man, that we may fight together. When Saul and all Israel heard those words of the Philistine, they were dismayed, and greatly afraid.

When Goliath the champion of the Philistines taunted the Israelites, he took over the airways and the atmosphere and released such fear that no one wanted to fight him. He released such fear and dread into the atmosphere until all the Israelites were scared just by what he was speaking? His words were producing a shift that caused the Israelites to coward. How many people do we know that do this, even in our own families?

When David came to the camp and heard Goliath, he was appalled by the shift Goliath was causing through his words.

Verse 26 - *And David spake to the men that stood by him, saying, what shall be done to the man that killeth this Philistine, and taketh away the reproach from Israel? For who is this uncircumcised Philistine, that he should defy the armies of the living God.*

<u>Reproach is Herpa in the Hebrew and means:</u>
1. Contumely, disgrace, rebuke, reproach (fully)
2. Shame, scorn taunt, scorn (upon enemy)
3. Reproach (resting upon condition of shame, disgrace or a reproach upon an object)

David could sense what was occurring in the atmosphere of the war camp and even in the region, just by listening to what Goliath was spewing. And it was not just in the atmosphere and region, as the definition lets us know that it was resting upon the Israelites. It literally became a physical condition and object of shame and reproach.

David first judged Goliath by stating that he had defied (blasphemed) the Lord and the Israelites and then performed three significant shifts to take Goliath down.
1. He first took five smooth stone and slung one hitting Goliath in the forehead (fivefold ministry)
2. Then he took Goliath's own sword and stabbed (executed) Goliath (David established what had taken place by planting his seed in the earth)

3. And then he cut his head off. (David solidified his work)

Prayers that shift God's judgment, grace, fire and glory into the earth:

2Chronicles 7:1-3 - Now when Solomon had made an end of praying, the fire came down from heaven, and consumed the burnt offering and the sacrifices; and the glory of the Lord filled the house. And the priests could not enter into the house of the Lord, because the glory of the Lord had filled the Lord's house. And when all the children of Israel saw how the fire came down, and the glory of the Lord upon the house, they bowed themselves with their faces to the ground upon the pavement, and worshipped, and praised the Lord, saying, for he is good; for his mercy endureth for ever.

The Message Version - *When Solomon finished praying, a bolt of lightning out of heaven struck the Whole-Burnt-Offering and sacrifices and the Glory of God filled The Temple. The Glory was so dense that the priests couldn't get in-- God so filled The Temple that there was no room for the priests! When all Israel saw the fire fall from heaven and the Glory of God fill The Temple, they fell on their knees, bowed their heads, and worshiped, thanking God: Yes! God is good! His love never quits!*

Prayer in this scripture is *Palal* and means:
1. To judge (officially or mentally); to intercede, pray
2. Entreat, judge, make supplication, to intervene, interpose

Solomon's prayers produced a consuming fire of God that judged the offerings and sacrifice he was offering to God, and shifted God's grace into his sphere of influence. When others witnessed the fire falling and the glory filling the temple, it triggered an effect of immediate worship unto the Lord.
WHEWWWWWW! SHIFT!

Personal consecration with the Lord in the holy place and unity in praise and worship that shifts in the awe striking glory of God:

> *2Chronicles 5:11-14 - And it came to pass, when the priests were come out of the holy place. For all the priests that were present were sanctified, and did not then wait by course: Also the Levites which were the singers, all of them of Asaph, of Heman, of Jeduthun, with their sons and their brethren, being arrayed in white linen, having cymbals and psalteries and harps, stood at the east end of the altar, and with them an hundred and twenty priests sounding with trumpets).*
>
> *It came even to pass, as the trumpeters and singers were as one, to make one sound to be heard in praising and thanking the Lord; and when they lifted up their voice with the trumpets and cymbals and instruments of musick, and praised the Lord, saying, for he is good; for his mercy endureth for ever: that then the house was filled with a cloud, even the house of the Lord; So that the priests could*

not stand to minister by reason of the cloud: for the glory of the Lord had filled the house of God.

The Message Version - *The priests then left the Holy Place. All the priests there were consecrated, regardless of rank or assignment; and all the Levites who were musicians were there--Asaph, Heman, Jeduthun, and their families, dressed in their worship robes; the choir and orchestra assembled on the east side of the Altar and were joined by 120 priests blowing trumpets.*

The choir and trumpets made one voice of praise and thanks to God --orchestra and choir in perfect harmony singing and playing praise to God: Yes! God is good! His loyal love goes on forever! Then a billowing cloud filled The Temple of God. The priests couldn't even carry out their duties because of the cloud--the glory of God! --that filled The Temple of God.

1Kings 8:10 - *And it came to pass, when the priests were come out of the holy place, that the cloud filled the house of the Lord, So that the priests could not stand to minister because of the cloud: for the glory of the Lord had filled the house of the Lord.*

Spend time with God and when you are truly transformed in His presence, you are endowed with power to SHIFT!
Praise, praise dance and singing praises that shifts God's judgment into the earth:

Psalms 149:3-9 - *Let them praise his name in the dance: let them sing praises unto him with the timbrel and harp. For the Lord taketh pleasure in his people: he will beautify the meek with salvation. Let the saints be joyful in glory: Let them sing aloud upon their beds. Let the high praises of God be in their mouth, and a twoedged sword in their hand;*

To execute vengeance upon the heathen, and punishments upon the people; to bind their kings with chains, and their nobles with fetters of iron; to execute upon them the judgment written: this honour have all his saints. Praise ye the Lord.

A high praise sets off an alarm while declaring the judgment of God. This type of shift causes an uprising.

<u>High</u> in the Hebrew is *Rowmĕmah* and means:
1. Uplifting
2. Arising

<u>The primitive root word of High is *Ruwa* and means:</u>

1. Shout, noise, alarm, cry, cry out, triumph, raise a sound, give a blast
2. To shout a war-cry or alarm of battle, to destroy
3. To sound a signal for war or march
4. To shout in triumph (over enemies), to shout in applause
5. To shout (with religious impulse), to cry out in distress
6. To utter a shout, a shout for joy, to shout in triumph, to shout for

Shift inside His power and praise Him!

> **Psalms 150** - *Praise Ye the Lord. Praise God in his sanctuary: Praise Him in the firmament of his power. Praise Him for his mighty acts: Praise Him according to his excellent greatness. Praise Him with the sound of the trumpet: Praise Him with the psaltery and harp.*
>
> *Praise Him with the timbrel and dance: Praise Him with stringed instruments and organs. Praise Him upon the loud cymbals: Praise Him upon the high*

sounding cymbals. Let everything that hath breath praise the Lord. Praise Ye the Lord.

Verse 1 The Amplified Version – Praise the Lord! Praise God in His sanctuary; praise Him in the heavens of His power!

<u>Praise in that scripture is *Halah* and means:</u>
1. To shine, to shine (fig. of God's favor), to flash forth light
2. To praise, boast, be boastful, boastful ones, boasters (participle)
3. To make a boast, glory, make one's boast, to be worthy of praise
4. To be praised, be made praiseworthy, be commended
5. To make a fool of, make into a fool, to act madly, act like a madman

- The word praise is a shifting command
- This is a global universal shift as the scriptures says *"let everything that has breath, praise Him."* Imagine a global praise of judgment going forth for God? WHEWWWW!!!!
- Such praise requires complete abandonment of self in boldly declaring the due adoration of the Lord. But not just to declare it, to boast His greatness while being so caught up in exalting Him, that the very praise itself jails the enemy, assault his land, and executes the judgments and plans of the Lord among people and nations

A shifting anointing that stirs up people and regions:

Jesus was a *Kingdom Shifter*. Often when people left His presence, they were searching out things He spoke, did and even just His very presence triggered devils, beliefs, inquiry in people and regions. Jesus was always impacting and even more effectively, He was known for performing miracles, signs and wonders. He was a *Kingdom Shifter* such that regions were transformed by His very presence. Jesus baffled and convicted people in towns where He was not well received. Because of their unbelief, He could only manifest a few miracles, but still caused a impactful shift.

> ***Mark 6:1-6*** - *Then He went out from there and came to His own country, and His disciples followed Him. And when the Sabbath had come, He began to teach in the synagogue. And many hearing Him were astonished, saying, "Where did this Man get these things? And what wisdom is this which is given to Him, that such mighty works are performed by His hands! Is this not the carpenter, the Son of Mary, and brother of James, Joses, Judas, and Simon? And are not His sisters here with us?" So they were offended at Him.*
>
> *But Jesus said to them, "A prophet is not without honor except in his own country, among his own relatives, and in his own house." Now He could do no mighty work there, except that He laid His hands on a few sick people and healed them. And He*

> *marveled because of their unbelief. Then He went about the villages in a circuit, teaching.*

Though the Jesus could only produce few miracles, the kingdom of God in Him offended people so much that it caused a shift in the region. Jesus left an impression that could be watered or at least put the people in remembrance that they were visited, yet rejected the Most High God. Jesus shook the place up, and even though many of the people were not receiving of Him, they knew a shift had occurred and were challenged by what they were experiencing to the point of offense. Even if they did not have a name or enlightenment on what they had experienced, they knew the glory that Jesus was carrying was unique to what they knew about Him and about God.

Further in this passage of scripture, we find that when Jesus released the disciples, He told them that if they are not received, to shake the dust off their shoes as testimony.

> **Verse 7-10** - *And He called the twelve to Himself, and began to send them out two by two, and gave them power over unclean spirits. He commanded them to take nothing for the journey except a staff— no bag, no bread, no copper in their money belts — but to wear sandals, and not to put on two tunics.*
>
> *Also He said to them, "In whatever place you enter a house, stay there till you depart from that place. [11] And whoever will not receive you nor hear*

you, when you depart from there, shake off the dust under your feet as a testimony against them. Assuredly, I say to you, it will be more tolerable for Sodom and Gomorrah in the day of judgment than for that city!"

Shake in the Greek is Ekinasso and means:
1. To Shake off so that something adhering shall fall
2. By this symbolic act, a person expresses extreme contempt for another, and refuses to have any further dealings with him
3. To shake off for (the cleansing of) one's self

What was falling off was judgment. The shaking of the shoe in this passage of scripture was a prophetic act that God's presence had come to visit the people, land, and region. The shaking (falling) of the dust from the shoes was a prophetic cleansing and prophetic establishment that God's presence had visited and despite being revealed the truth, they had refused Him and thus would be judged for their actions once Jesus revisited the earth. For Jesus expressed further in this passage of scripture, that Sodom and Gomorrah would receive more grace than those cities that had received a shaking of dust for refusing the kingdom of God.

When one carries a true shifters' anointing or releases a word that something is shifting, what he are she is releasing is judgment. That judgment may be against the enemy, judgment regarding the person or people, or the judgment for the release of God's kingdom and truth to manifest in a people or within that church, business, sphere or region. When you are operating as a kingdom shifter, you are overriding the void and darkness and establishing the kingdom of God in its place. SHIFT!

Kingdom Realities of Shifting

"Kingdom Realities Of Shifting With God," examines God's reasons, purposes and plans of SHIFTING and transitioning us throughout destiny; while exploring the grief, loss, shock, trauma, deliverance, healing, benefits and blessings that occur as we SHIFT and live in the continual momentum of God.

> **Psalms 16:11** - *Thou wilt shew me the path of life: in thy presence is fulness of joy; at thy right hand there are pleasures for evermore.*

When God says SHIFT! Ask questions while you are SHIFTING with Him! If you remain stagnant you cannot comprehend Him through the frustrations caused by your disobedience. If you SHIFT with Him, peace in your obedience will help to map the plan and will for your life & even bring to your memory, courage, guidance and revelation He has already said and has already hid in your heart.

Though your obedience may bring peace, and you will have some revelation and guidance of the reason you are SHIFTING, sometimes you will not understand or be able to explain or put words what you are experiencing when SHIFTING. Also you may lack revelation as to how past seasons and experiences impact or connect to the SHIFT. The most pertinent information you may have is to SHIFT with God. JUST SHIFT! You may also have a knowing in your Spirit that this SHIFT is critical and if you do not SHIFT you could spiritual die or be stifled. When you have this JUST SHIFT! There are other instances where you may not even be aware that a SHIFT is necessary, yet God is requiring you to SHIFT. In addition there can be instances that a SHIFT is occurring and you may not be aware until things have started to transition in your life. Resist resisting and SHIFT!

> ***Isaiah 14:24*** - *The LORD Almighty has sworn, "Surely, as I have planned, so it will be, and as I have purposed, so it will happen.*

God has planned and purposed destiny for our lives and He has sworn to complete His work. The word *"sworn"* means a declared vow or oath has been taken. When we give our lives to God we come into covenant with His plans and purposes. So though His SHIFTS have plans and purposes, they can come at any time without us really grasping what He is doing.

> ***Isaiah 55:8-11*** - *For My thoughts are not your thoughts, neither are your ways My ways, says the Lord. For as the heavens are higher than the earth, so are My ways higher than your ways and My thoughts than your thoughts.*
>
> *For as the rain and snow come down from the heavens, and return not there again, but water the earth and make it bring forth and sprout, that it may give seed to the sower and bread to the eater, So shall My word be that goes forth out of My mouth: it shall not return to Me void [without producing any effect, useless], but it shall accomplish that*

which I please and purpose, and it shall prosper in the thing for which I sent it.

<u>Thoughts</u> in the Hebrew is <u>Machanshebeth</u> and means:
1. Contrivance (an obvious or forced plan or mechanical device)
2. A texture, machine, or (abstractly) intention
3. Plan (whether bad, a plot; or good, advice)
4. Cunning (work), curious work, device (- sed),
5. Imagination, invented, means, purpose, thought

Through this passage of scripture, we discern that that God will make decisions, changes, SHIFTS that we may not comprehend. Because God's thoughts are devices - literal machines and inventions, they can serve as SHIFTS in our lives. They will occur because they are a part of the voice and will of God activating and moving in our lives. This passage, however, does not say we cannot have God's thoughts and ways. We are also reminded that God reveals His mysteries to His people and if we seek, ask, and knock, we will be provided with what we are pursuing.

> **Amos 3:7** - *Surely the Lord GOD will do nothing, but he revealeth his secret unto his servants the prophets.*
> **John 15:15** - *I no longer call you servants, because a servant does not know his master's business. Instead, I have called you friends, for everything that I learned from my Father I have made known to you.*

> *Mark 4:11* - *And he said unto them, unto you it is given to know the mystery of the kingdom of God: but unto them that are without, all these things are done in parables.*

> *Mark 7:7* - *Ask, and it shall be given you; seek, and ye shall find; knock, and it shall be opened unto you: For every one that asketh receiveth; and he that seeketh findeth; and to him that knocketh it shall be opened.*

Some things God will share in detail. Sometimes He may require us to walk by faith and/or a spiritual knowing and then share later or over time. God has His reasons for how He shares information with us as even in His revealing methods are a part of His thoughts, plans and will for our lives. The words "*ask, seek, and knock*" require constant pursuit, while creating a constant dependence, surrendering, and dialog of continual communication and interactions with God. God is making sure we remain connected to Him so He can be actively and continually involved in our lives, so we can have relationship with Him, and so we can continually SHIFT into His will and ordained purpose. This is the reason God tells us to walk by faith. Faith builds relationship with God and relinquishes the burden of our lives to Him. The more we realize that not knowing everything or always understanding God is not a punishment but draws us closer to Him, the easier it will be to SHIFT with Him and live a sold out lifestyle with Him. As you SHIFT and live in God's momentum, revelation and understanding begins to unfold as you SHIFT and further grow in relationship and intimacy with Him. God will guide your every step as you trust Him, learn Him and SHIFT.

Releasing The Old When Shifting

> *Isaiah 49:18-19* - *Remember ye not the former things, neither consider the things of old. Behold, I will do a new thing; now it shall spring forth; shall ye not know it? I will even make a way in the wilderness, and rivers in the desert.*
>
> **The Message Version** - *Do not call to mind the former things, or ponder things of the past. "Behold, I will do something new, now it will spring forth; will you not be aware of it? I will even make a roadway in the wilderness, Rivers in the desert.*

This does not mean we won't remember the old. The scripture is telling us not to dwell on the old or to keep reliving the old. If it crosses our mind that is one thing but to bring it to our remembrance and constantly dwell on it is a whole other matter.

Continuously recounting, remembering, thinking on, recalling, mentioning the new keeps us tormented and stuck in the past, and hinders is from fully embracing the new. It is like a tape recorder that we have on repeat. We keep hitting play to hear our favorite song, favorite word, and favorite experience. The memory becomes a high place and idolatrous in our lives.

> *2Corinthians 10:5* - *Casting down imaginations, and every high thing that exalteth itself against the knowledge of God, and bringing into captivity every thought to the obedience of Christ.*

The memories, imaginations, and desires of the old season becomes the God that drives us rather than us living in momentum with our God that is SHIFTING us to the new.

Isaiah 49:18-19 lets us know that as we SHIFT, a springing up is going to take place. This springing up can be subtle or it can be shocking. The word encourages us to "*Behold*" - "*be aware*" of this springing up. We are to "*Behold*" because as we SHIFT, this springing up is inevitable. This uprising pushes out the old while manifesting the new. The old things do not SHIFT with us or do not work, and we do not quite understand the new that is manifesting in and around us. God wants us to be aware of this and to know that the loss and shock we may experience is part of the SHIFT. He wants this to be common knowledge - **BEHOLD!** - so we can discern that this is occurring and it is a natural process of SHIFTING with Him.

One key to letting go of the old when SHIFTING is to cleanse your memories. Especially those memories that have power over your thoughts and emotions and cause you to recycle in the old. Also break soul ties with experiences and people of the past and command your memories to become testimonies of what you have accomplished and overcome.

Dictionary.com defines *Triggers* as:
1. A device, as a lever, the pulling or pressing of which releases a detent or spring
2. Anything, as an act or event that serves as a stimulus and initiates or precipitates a reaction or series of reactions.

Triggers can be past painful experiences. Triggers also can be good times, fun times, sinful fun times (cause uhmmmm sin has its pleasure), etc. If a memory draws you back into constantly dwelling and yearning for those experiences, then there is a possibility that this memory has exalted or SHIFTED to lust or idolatry rather than admiration to which you simply admiring a memory or heartfelt experience. If this is occurring then that lust or idol needs to be cleansed out of the soul, heart, emotions, and appetite, so that it will not keep seducing you back into old things and desires that God is saying to let go of.

- Cleanse these triggers by using the blood of Jesus and the healing power of God
- Repent for any sins that are attached to the memories
- Share your hurts with God as it relates to those memories and release forgiveness where necessary
- Be sure to cleanse any anger, resentment, disappointment, fear, bitterness, etc. that maybe holding you bondage to that memory.

- Command your memories to be healed, sealed and testimonies of things you have accomplished and overcome

Philippians 3:12-14 - *Not that I have already obtained this or am already perfect, but I press on to make it my own, because Christ Jesus has made me his own. Brothers, I do not consider that I have made it my own. But one thing I do: forgetting what lies behind and straining forward to what lies ahead, I press on toward the goal for the prize of the upward call of God in Christ Jesus.*

Proverbs 4:25-27 - *Let your eyes look directly forward, and your gaze be straight before you. Ponder the path of your feet; then all your ways will be sure. Do not swerve to the right or to the left; turn your foot away from evil.*

Proverbs 28:13 - *Whoever conceals his transgressions will not prosper, but he who confesses and forsakes them will obtain mercy.*

Philippians 4:8-9 - *Finally, brothers, whatever is true, whatever is honorable, whatever is just, whatever is pure, whatever is lovely, whatever is commendable, if there is any excellence, if there is anything worthy of praise, think about these things. What you have learned and received and heard and seen in me — practice these things, and the God of peace will be with you.*

The Realities Of Loss Shock & Trauma In The Shift

While you are SHIFTING with God be okay with going through the natural grieving process of what you have left or loss. Break soul ties with anything that needs to be destroyed in you that will make you dread going with God and that will try to pull you back to a place He is SHIFTING you out of. This is what caused Lots wife to turn into a pillar of salt. She was enmeshed with the old season, old ways, old wounds, and old sins, until she could not receive the cleansing, freedom, and healing that came with the new abundant place that was ahead of her. TRUST JESUS & SHIFT!

> *Isaiah 58:11 - And the LORD shall guide thee continually, and satisfy thy soul in drought, and make fat thy bones: and thou shalt be like a watered garden, and like a spring of water, whose waters fail not.*
>
> *Hebrews 10:38 - Now the just shall live by faith: but if any man draw back, my soul shall have no pleasure in him.*
>
> *Genesis 19:23-26 - The sun was risen upon the earth when Lot entered into Zoar. Then the Lord rained upon Sodom and upon Gomorrah brimstone and fire from the Lord out of heaven; and he overthrew those cities, and all the plain, and all the inhabitants of the cities, and that which grew upon*

> *the ground. But his wife looked back from behind him, and she became a pillar of salt.*

You will loose things and people when you SHIFT with God. You will loose things and people that you never thought you would have had to give up or that had to be terminated from your life. You will feel hurt, abandoned, lonely due to loosing some things and people. And at times you will be shocked by some of the things and people you have to leave behind.

Some experiences of shock will come from the lack of support by those people and things you thought were for you and necessary for the journey. You will be like *"What The What???"* Some of the shock will come from the turbulence and changes experienced in the SHIFT! The other challenge is because you are on a continual journey, you may experience multiple shocks before you process toward and settle into your new place in God.

> **2Corinthians 5:17-18** - *Therefore if any man be in Christ, he is a new creature: old things are passed away; behold, all things are become new. And all things are of God, who hath reconciled us to himself by Jesus Christ, and hath given to us the ministry of reconciliation.*

In this passage of scripture, God clearly lets us know that some things that are old die, are neglected, transgress (violated or offended), averted (pass by or aside from, warded off), when we SHIFT to the new.

He blatantly says "passed away" like there is nothing to it. However we know when that with a passing comes grief, loss, and shock.

Moreover, new things are springing up in, for, around, and through you which can be a shock. Some things and some people are pushed out when the new springs up! This does not necessarily make these things or people bad or make relinquishing the old easy. God is in control of the SHIFT and He determines what springs up and what is pushed out.

<u>In explaining that occurs in the Shift, Dictionary.com defines *Shock* as:</u>
1. A sudden and violent blow or impact; collision
2. A sudden or violent disturbance or commotion: the shock of battle
3. A sudden or violent disturbance of the mind, emotions, or sensibilities
4. The cause of such a disturbance: The rebuke came as a shock
5. Pathology. a collapse of circulatory function, caused by severe injury, blood loss, or disease, and characterized by pallor, sweating, weak pulse, and very low blood pressure. Compare anaphylactic shock, cardiogenic shock, hypovolemic shock
6. The physiological effect produced by the passage of an electric current through the body
7. To strike or jar with intense surprise, horror, disgust, etc.

When someone goes into shock the brain has grasped a revelation that something has changed and is causing pain, damage, panic or awe in the spiritual or natural body. The brain feels like a life threatening change has occurred and goes into lock down - shut down mode. In the natural body the blood stops flowing to the major organs. In the spiritual sense, it's like your air supply cuts off and you feel breathless and helpless because the shock has caused an interruption in your ability to feel safe, secure, confident, loved, and trusting. These are all major attributes a person needs in order to continue SHIFTING in the momentum of a God, yet we tend to want them from what is familiar rather than from the new supplied to us. Just like in the natural shock experience, you feel like you are going to die and fail or that you have already died or fallen because of what has happened to you and what you have experience.

One key to handling shock is to know that if you are truly experiencing a SHIFT, you are going to have shock. In a SHIFT you are moving from one place to another. Some of the synonyms of the word SHIFT are as followed:

Alteration
Bend
Displacement
Change
Conversion
Deflection
Deviation

Fluctuation
Modification
Movement
Passage
Rearrangement
Removal
Shifting
Substitution
Switch
Transfer
Transference
Transformation
Transition
Translocation
Variation
Veerin

We like to think that SHIFTING entails a smooth path but that is a false delusion we trick ourselves into believing so we can embrace the SHIFT. SHIFTING definitely entails a path but it has many steeps and hills and pathways and to conquer. Even a newly built path or trail can have rocks, sticks, breezy scary trees, squirrels and other lurking animals, side walk bumps, curves, and even hills built into its passageway. So it is a part of the process for things to catch us off guard as we SHIFT, thus causing some shock and awe.

Just like we are taken to the hospital for shock that occurs in the natural. We must take our spiritual shock to God and let Him do emergency healing and restoration on us. With the experience of shock a level of trauma occurs. This trauma must be cleansed out so we can properly heal from shock and continue on in our journey.

When trauma from shock is not dealt with, it causes unhealed wounds, physical illnesses, and can even cause a spirit of fear to root in our soul and heart. We will have challenges further SHIFTING due to being paralyzed inside our shocking experience. The world of psychology calls this post-traumatic stress disorder (PTSD). PTSD is an anxiety disorder that manifests after you have gone through an extreme emotional trauma that involved the threat of injury or death. We must go to God and be honest about our feelings and let Him cleanse of from the turbulence experienced in our SHIFT.

When you SHIFT not only do things and people change but you change. Things in you will change that you did not know needed changing. God will require changes that you do not even think you can accomplish or that are necessary. You will wonder *what was the purpose of the past seasons and experiences if they cannot go where you are going.* You will wonder *how can I SHIFT and change at the same time.* It will feel like double duty at times - you SHIFTING and you are changing - you are SHIFTING and being delivered - you are SHIFTING and you are healing - you are SHIFTING and being delivered and healed while still having to live, take care day to day things, and SHIFT and deliver, heal and help others.

The Process of A Destiny Shift

When you are aligning with God, especially in a destiny shift, anything that is unhealthy will be exposed or pushed out as you shift.

- People and demons will manifest
- The truth of who people are will be exposed
- Betrayals may occur as you may break bread and be denied by the very ones that will separate from you during the most significant part of your shift.
- Those around you may compete for position and titles in your life and ministry. They are focused on what they can benefit from your transition more so than being a support and servant to you as you shift and transition into destiny.
- Any weakness, insecurity, or fear in you and others in your mists, will be exposed
- Grief and heaviness may come upon you due to the weight of the destiny shift
- You may be mocked, ridiculed, while your identity appears to be harassed and stripped.
- People will try to get you to defend yourself, God and even use ridicule and blasphemy to get you to abort your shift.
- Those that betray you may end up aborting their position in your life and in their own destiny because of the grief and shame their actions.

- Those things and people that need to be revealed to help you further align with God's shift will manifest so that you will be able to fulfill God's purpose in a healthy and pure manner.

When the season came for Jesus to die on the cross for mankind, the unhealthiness among His disciples was exposed.

Jesus still blesses, breaks bread with, and honors those that will betray Him during The most intricate part of His shift. He reveals what will happen and they deny it and contend they would die for Him. There words speak an unwavering love but their actions lack the truth of one laying down his life for a friend - a savior.

> *Luke 22-19-23 - And he took bread, and gave thanks, and brake it, and gave unto them, saying, this is my body which is given for you: this do in remembrance of me. Likewise also the cup after supper, saying, this cup is the new testament in my blood, which is shed for you.*
>
> *But, behold, the hand of him that betrayeth me is with me on the table. And truly the Son of man goeth, as it was determined:but woe unto that man by whom he is betrayed! And they began to enquire among themselves, which of them it was that should do this thing.*

Those around Jesus began to compete for position and accolades rather than be discerning of the hour that was at hand.

> *Luke 22:24-27 - And there was also a strife among them, which of them should be accounted the greatest. And he said unto them, the kings of the Gentiles exercise lordship over them; and they that exercise authority upon them are called benefactors. But ye shall not be so: but he that is greatest among you, let him be as the younger; and he that is chief, as he that doth serve. For whether is greater, he that sitteth at meat, or he that serveth? is not he that sitteth at meat? But I am among you as he that serveth.*

Jesus recognized that Peter needed intercession because the enemy desired to sift Peter like wheat and Peter was not strong enough to endure the sifting or the shift that was coming.

> *Luke 22:31-35 - And the Lord said, Simon, Simon, behold, Satan hath desired to have you, that he may sift you as wheat: But I have prayed for thee, that thy faith fail not: and when thou art converted, strengthen thy brethren. And he said unto him, Lord, I am ready to go with thee, both into prison, and to death. And he said, I tell thee, Peter, the cock shall not crow this day, before that thou shalt thrice deny that thou knowest me.*

Though Jesus was not weak, fearful or insecure, He was grieved unto death and ask God to remove His cup of destiny, due to the weight of having to die for the sins of the world.

> ***Matthew 26-36-39*** - *Then cometh Jesus with them unto a place called Gethsemane, and saith unto the disciples, Sit ye here, while I go and pray yonder. And he took with him Peter and the two sons of Zebedee, and began to be sorrowful and very heavy. Then saith he unto them, my soul is exceeding sorrowful, even unto death: tarry ye here, and watch with me. And he went a little further, and fell on his face, and prayed, saying, O my Father, if it be possible, let this cup pass from me: nevertheless not as I will, but as thou wilt.*

> ***Luke 22:40-44*** - *And when he was at the place, he said unto them, Pray that ye enter not into temptation. And he was withdrawn from them about a stone's cast, and kneeled down, and prayed, Saying, Father, if thou be willing, remove this cup from me: nevertheless not my will, but thine, be done. And there appeared an angel unto him from heaven, strengthening him. And being in an agony he prayed more earnestly: and his sweat was as it were great drops of blood falling down to the ground.*

Disciples kept falling asleep in the garden. Their spirit was willing but their flesh was not surrendered and dead enough to go where Jesus was going.

> ***Matthew 26:40-46*** - *And he cometh unto the disciples, and findeth them asleep, and saith unto Peter, What, could ye not watch with me one hour?*

> *Watch and pray, that ye enter not into temptation: the spirit indeed is willing, but the flesh is weak. He went away again the second time, and prayed, saying, O my Father, if this cup may not pass away from me, except I drink it, thy will be done. And he came and found them asleep again: for their eyes were heavy. And he left them, and went away again, and prayed the third time, saying the same words. Then cometh he to his disciples, and saith unto them, Sleep on now, and take your rest: behold, the hour is at hand, and the Son of man is betrayed into the hands of sinners. Rise, let us be going: behold, he is at hand that doth betray me.*

Judas was one of the disciples that was with Jesus at the last super but he betrayed Jesus with a kiss and sold Jesus out for money. He then ended up killing Himself due being overcome with shame and guilt from his actions.

> **Matthew 26-47-50** - *And while he yet spake, lo, Judas, one of the twelve, came, and with him a great multitude with swords and staves, from the chief priests and elders of the people. Now he that betrayed him gave them a sign, saying, Whomsoever I shall kiss, that same is he: hold him fast. And forthwith he came to Jesus, and said, Hail, master; and kissed him. And Jesus said unto him, Friend, wherefore art thou come? Then came they, and laid hands on Jesus, and took him.*

Peter became hot tempered and cut off a soldier's ear.

> **Matthew 26:51-52** - *And, behold, one of them which were with Jesus stretched out his hand, and drew his sword, and struck a servant of the high*

> *priest's, and smote off his ear. Then said Jesus unto him, Put up again thy sword into his place: for all they that take the sword shall perish with the sword.*

Religion, tradition, leaders, legislation, demon powers and principalities will rise up against you when there is a destiny shift occurring in your life.

> *Luke 22:52-53 - Then Jesus said unto the chief priests, and captains of the temple, and the elders, which were come to him, Be ye come out, as against a thief, with swords and staves? When I was daily with you in the temple, ye stretched forth no hands against me: but this is your hour, and the power of darkness.*

Peter denied Jesus three times.

> ***Luke 22:54-62*** *- Then took they him, and led him, and brought him into the high priest's house. And Peter followed afar off. And when they had kindled a fire in the midst of the hall, and were set down together, Peter sat down among them. But a certain maid beheld him as he sat by the fire, and earnestly looked upon him, and said, This man was also with him. And he denied him, saying, Woman, I know him not. And after a little while another saw him, and said, Thou art also of them. And Peter said, Man, I am not.*
>
> *And about the space of one hour after another confidently affirmed, saying, Of a truth this fellow also was with him: for he is a Galilaean. And Peter said, Man, I know not what thou sayest. And*

> *immediately, while he yet spake, the cock crew. And the Lord turned, and looked upon Peter. And Peter remembered the word of the Lord, how he had said unto him, Before the cock crow, thou shalt deny me thrice. And Peter went out, and wept bitterly.*

Jesus was mocked for His beliefs and His beliefs and identity and calling was brought into question in effort to get Him to defend and even save Himself from the shift.

> **Luke 22:63-71** - *And the men that held Jesus mocked him, and smote him. And when they had blindfolded him, they struck him on the face, and asked him, saying, Prophesy, who is it that smote thee? And many other things blasphemously spake they against him. And as soon as it was day, the elders of the people and the chief priests and the scribes came together, and led him into their council, saying,-- Art thou the Christ? tell us.*
>
> *And he said unto them, if I tell you, ye will not believe: And if I also ask you, ye will not answer me, nor let me go. Hereafter shall the Son of man sit on the right hand of the power of God. Then said they all, Art thou then the Son of God? And he said unto them, Ye say that I am. And they said, what need we any further witness? For we ourselves have heard of his own mouth.*

Judas kills himself after recognizing the consequences to His actions against Jesus.

> *Matthew 27:3 - Then Judas, which had betrayed him, when he saw that he was condemned, repented himself, and brought again the thirty pieces of silver to the chief priests and elders, Saying, I have sinned in that I have betrayed the innocent blood. And they said, what is that to us? See thou to that. And he cast down the pieces of silver in the temple, and departed, and went and hanged himself.*

Like Jesus when transition in a shift, it is important for us to know when to hold our piece and when to speak or act. It is important to discern what situations are a part of the processing of your shift, what is your battle, and what is working an exceedingly greater weight of glory for you as you shift.

> *Matthew 26:61-68 - And the high priest arose, and said unto him, answerest thou nothing? What is it which these witness against thee? But Jesus held his peace. And the high priest answered and said unto him, I adjure thee by the living God, that thou tell us whether thou be the Christ, the Son of God. Jesus saith unto him, Thou hast said: nevertheless I say unto you, hereafter shall ye see the Son of man sitting on the right hand of power, and coming in the clouds of heaven priest rent his clothes, saying, He hath spoken blasphemy; what further need have we of witnesses? Behold, now ye have heard his blasphemy. What think ye? They answered and said, He is guilty of death. Then did they spit in his face, and buffeted him; and others smote him with the palms of their hands, Saying, Prophesy unto us, thou Christ, Who is he that smote thee?*

Matthew 27:11-14 - *And Jesus stood before the governor: and the governor asked him, saying, Art thou the King of the Jews? And Jesus said unto him, Thou sayest. And when he was accused of the chief priests and elders, he answered nothing. Then said Pilate unto him, hearest thou not how many things they witness against thee? And he answered him to never a word; insomuch that the governor marvelled greatly.*

Matthew 27:28-31 - *And they stripped him, and put on him a scarlet robe. And when they had platted a crown of thorns, they put it upon his head, and a reed in his right hand:and they bowed the knee before him, and mocked him, saying, Hail, King of the Jews! And they spit upon him, and took the reed, and smote him on the head. And after that they had mocked him, they took the robe off from him, and put his own raiment on him, and led him away to crucify him.*

Matthew 26:39-43 - And they that passed by reviled him, wagging their heads, and saying, Thou that destroyest the temple, and buildest it in three days, save thyself. If thou be the Son of God, come down from the cross. Likewise also the chief priests mocking Him, with the scribes and elders, said, He saved others; Himself He cannot save. If He be the King of Israel, let Him now come down from the cross, and we will believe Him. He trusted in God; let him deliver him now, if he will have him: for he said, I am the Son of God.

When Jesus was on the cross in His defying moment within the shift, it was just Him and God. Though on inquisitors and spectators remained, all that was unhealthy and familiar in Jesus life, had been removed so He could operate in the pure truth of His identity and calling.

> ***Matthew 27:46-49*** - *And about the ninth hour Jesus cried with a loud voice, saying, Eli, Eli, lama sabachthani? That is to say, My God, my God, why hast thou forsaken me? Some of them that stood there, when they heard that, said, this man calleth for Elias. Some of them that stood there, when they heard that, said, this man calleth for Elias. And straightway one of them ran, and took a spunge, and filled it with vinegar, and put it on a reed, and gave him to drink. The rest said, Let be, let us see whether Elias will come to save him.*

When Jesus cried aloud, He produced a travailing sound that birthed forth the shift. Though to others He died, Jesus actually released a judgment that manifested the shift of destiny that was occurring in the spirit, in the earth realm.

> ***Matthew 27:50-53*** - *Jesus, when he had cried again with a loud voice, yielded up the ghost. And, behold, the veil of the temple was rent in twain from the top to the bottom; and the earth did quake, and the rocks rent; and the graves were opened; and many bodies of the saints which slept arose, and came out of the graves after his resurrection, and went into the holy city, and appeared unto many.*

As the shift occurs, many that once denied and mocked you, will then begin to believe and fear who God is in you.

> ***Matthew 27:54*** *- Now when the centurion, and they that were with him, watching Jesus, saw the earthquake, and those things that were done, they feared greatly, saying, Truly this was the Son of God.*

When there is a destiny shift, though at times we feel grieved or like we are dying, there is always a rising into newness. Jesus rose from His shifting grave in three days. He fulfilled prophecy that had been spoken over His life even before His birth and journey on earth.

> ***Matthew 28:3-6*** *- And, behold, there was a great earthquake: for the angel of the Lord descended from heaven, and came and rolled back the stone from the door, and sat upon it.-- His countenance was like lightning, and his raiment white as snow: And for fear of him the keepers did shake, and became as dead men. And the angel answered and said unto the women, Fear not ye: for I know that ye seek Jesus, which was crucified. He is not here: for he is risen, as he said. Come, see the place where the Lord lay.*

God will allow you to appear to those who:

Walked With You

Matthew 28:9 - *And as they went to tell his disciples, behold, Jesus met them, saying, All hail. And they came and held him by the feet, and worshipped him. Then said Jesus unto them, Be not afraid: go tell my brethren that they go into Galilee, and there shall they see me.*

Hurt You and Mocked You
Matthew 28:11-15 - *Now when they were going, behold, some of the watch came into the city, and shewed unto the chief priests all the things that were done. And when they were assembled with the elders, and had taken counsel, they gave large money unto the soldiers, Saying, Say ye, His disciples came by night, and stole him away while we slept. And if this come to the governor's ears, we will persuade him, and secure you. So they took the money, and did as they were taught: and this saying is commonly reported among the Jews until this day.*
Refused to Believe or Accept You
Matthew 28:16-18 - *Then the eleven disciples went away into Galilee, into a mountain where Jesus had appointed them. And when they saw him, they worshipped him: but some doubted. And Jesus came and spake unto them, saying, all power is given unto me in heaven and in earth.*

Reconcile with some that may have denied and deserted you and even release them into their destiny.
John 21:15-17 - *So when they had dined, Jesus saith to Simon Peter, Simon, son of Jonas, lovest thou me more than these? He saith unto him, Yea, Lord; thou knowest that I love thee. He saith unto him, Feed my lambs. He saith to him again the second time, Simon, son of Jonas, lovest thou me? He saith unto him, Yea, Lord; thou knowest that I love thee. He saith unto him, Feed my sheep. He saith unto him the third time, Simon, son of Jonas, lovest thou me? Peter*

was grieved because he said unto him the third time, Lovest thou me? And he said unto him, Lord, thou knowest all things; thou knowest that I love thee. Jesus saith unto him, Feed my sheep.

Accept the process of destiny and/or significant transitions! SHIFT!

Fearless Immovable Decree

Scripture References: 2Corinthians 4:8-16, Acts 20:22-24, 1Corinthians 4:10-14, Romans 8:32-37, Isaiah 59:17-19

- Flesh don't move me
- Bad attitudes don't move me
- Intimidating and defying tactics of Goliath don't move me
- Jezebel's seductive and raging rants don't move me
- Backstabbing words and actions don't move me
- Betrayal don't move me
- Gossip, slander, and demonic chatter don't move me
- Misunderstandings and misjudgments; even when people just don't get it, get me - that don't move me
- Ridicule don't move me
- Lies don't move me
- False or manipulating burdens don't move me
- Rejection and the rejection issues of others don't move me
- Hatred. jealousy, competition, and covetousness doesn't move me
- Abandonment and people leaving don't move me
- Having to be lonely and journey in God alone doesn't move me
- Witches and witchcraft don't move me

- Demonic floods, winds, and storms don't move me
- Warfare and demonic visitations don't move me
- Trials, tribulation and persecution don't move me
- Devils and angry principalities and powers show don't move me
- The hounds of hell don't move me and can't stop me
- Death and being a martyr for Christ don't move me
- For I am fixed, secure, stable, moored (to secure, fix firmly) in Jesus!
- I am anchored, rooted, braced, set firm, set fast, perfectly jammed, stiff and stuck to the truth of Jesus.
- I am not budging, motionless to the things of the world and to Satan, unmoving, immobile, rooted in a stationary in Jesus
- I am remaining still, stock-still, not moving a muscle, rooted to the spot, transfixed, paralyzed in God's presence and will, frozen, fastened, locked, locked in, unwavering! I am immovable in Jesus!

Satan does not like harmony. He does not like unity or people agreeing. *Ezekiel 28:13-18* contends that Satan was an anointed cherub, full of beautiful stones and perfect in sound from creation, until iniquity - disharmony was found in Him.

> *Ezekiel 28:13-18 - Thou hast been in Eden the garden of God; every precious stone was thy covering, the sardius, topaz, and the diamond, the beryl, the onyx, and the jasper, the sapphire, the emerald, and the carbuncle, and gold: the workmanship of thy tabrets and of thy pipes was prepared in thee in the day that thou wast created. Thou art the anointed cherub that covereth; and I have set thee so: thou wast upon the holy mountain of God; thou hast walked up and down in the midst of the stones of fire. Thou wast perfect in thy ways from the day that thou wast created, till iniquity was found in thee.*
>
> *By the multitude of thy merchandise they have filled the midst of thee with violence, and thou hast sinned: therefore I will cast thee as profane out of the mountain of God: and I will destroy thee, O covering cherub, from the midst of the stones of fire. Thine heart was lifted up because of thy beauty, thou hast corrupted thy wisdom by reason of thy brightness: I will cast thee to the ground, I will lay thee before kings, that they may behold thee. Thou hast defiled thy sanctuaries by the multitude of thine iniquities, by the iniquity of thy traffick;*

therefore will I bring forth a fire from the midst of thee, it shall devour thee, and I will bring thee to ashes upon the earth in the sight of all them that behold thee.

This passage of scripture reveals that God responds to disharmony, but not by agreeing and releasing that which we have forbidden or decreed. As when there is disharmony, His response is judgment.

> **Psalms 133** - *Behold, how good and how pleasant it is for brethren to dwell together in unity! It is like the precious oil upon the head, running down on the beard, the beard of Aaron, Running down on the edge of his garments. It is like the dew of Hermon, Descending upon the mountains of Zion; for there the Lord commanded the blessing – Life forevermore.*
>
> **Verse 2 The Amplified Version** - *It is like the precious ointment poured on the head, that ran down on the beard, even the beard of Aaron [the first high priest], that came down upon the collar and skirts of his garments [consecrating the whole body].*

The scripture encourages us to come to attention by beholding how good and how pleasant it is for brethren to dwell together in unity. The word:

- **Good** denotes that there is wealth and potential present

- ***Pleasant*** denotes an enjoyment, a delight, an agreement and even that an agreeing atmospheric sound is present (Where there is chaos and division, the agreement and atmospheric sound is erratic)
- ***Brethren*** denotes that we are all in relationship with one another and that we resemble one another in some fashion or likeness

Dictionary.com defines *Unity* as:
1. The state of being one; oneness
2. A whole or totality as combining all its parts into one.
3. The state or fact of being united or combined into one, as of the parts of a whole; unification.
4. Absence of diversity; unvaried or uniform character.
5. Oneness of mind, feeling, etc., as among a number of persons
6. Concord, harmony, or agreement

The Psalms not only tells us to unify, but to dwell together in unity.

The word ***dwell*** denotes a continual occurrence that has no ending.

The Hebrew word for ***dwell*** is "*yasab*" and means "*to inhabit, abide, remain, to sit, to stay, and also to marry.*"

Though, we know the importance of unity as it relates to gathering together, having like hearts, mindsets, visions, giftings, etc., we never really consider the concept of unity being one of a great bond where we stay among one another and in tune with one another to a degree of marriage - of covenant. This definitely yields revelation of the reason worldly gangs and cults have blood in-blood out covenants. The agreement is essentially equated to giving yourself to marriage – hmmmm - and marriage is for life - the unity has no earthly end. Generally one marries in life and until death.

Spiritually the concept of being married to a group does not mean remaining bonded to that group forever, but as God places a person in that ministry, one should be dedicated to God's purpose and be a blessing to the ministry. I guess we could contend that there should be a mindset of spiritual connectedness in relations to exuding the love, unity and respect portrayed in a marriage. God should be the head, the leader should be submitted, hear and obey God, and the people should follow the leader as he or she hears and follow God. This would help avoid groups within the church or ministries from becoming a cult or cultic in nature and characteristics. This would also assist with helping to sustain and maintaining the harmony of a group such that even when challenges arise, discord, confusion, etc., is quickly dismantled. I say this because if the covenant is properly followed with God being the head, then everything else begins to align with His plan, will, nature and character.

Psalms 133 compares the dwelling of unity to a precious anointing oil running down the body of Aaron.

Aaron was the older brother of Moses who assisted with leading the Israelites out of Egypt. He was eloquent in speech, prophet of God and miracles, signs and wonders followed his ministry. He performed these miracles with his walking stick, changing it one time into a serpent and another into blossoms and almonds. Also, by stretching out his walking stick at the request of Moses, he brought on the first three plagues: blood, frogs, and lice; and, in cooperation with Moses, he produced the sixth plague, boils, and the eighth plague, locusts.

Aaron represented the priestly functions of his tribe, becoming the first High Priest of the Israelites (Exodus 6:16-20, 7:7). High Priest were in charge of the Temple (or tabernacle) worship.

As the Psalms explores the fruit of dwelling in unity, we see that the anointing saturated Aaron from head, beard, and onto the skirts of his garment.

Now in my supernatural thinking, I would discern that the Psalms writer David, making this significant indication of the anointing flowing down to Aaron's skirt, was a representation of spiritual borders, or a regional outpouring of the anointing oil. Skirt – border – hem – edge - hmmmmm?? But we will just ponder that revelation and explore it further later in our study.

The Psalms then says dwelling in unity is like the dew of Hermon, descending upon the mountains of Zion.

The word *dew* denotes a tangible mist or covering that is released to refresh (moisten) in some vegetative fashion.

The Christian Worldview Journal states the following:
> *The dew from Mount Hermon doesn't literally fall on Mount Zion. Mount Hermon lies over 100 miles northeast of Jerusalem. With a height of over 9,000 feet, it is the highest mountain in the region and is often snow-capped. Mount Hermon was lush throughout the year with heavy dew, while Mount Zion was desperately dry during the summer months when no rain fell at all. Two of the annual religious festivals fell during these months, so most pilgrims encountered a dry and dusty Jerusalem. But their unity seemed to transform the place! It was so wonderful that it was as if the dew of Mount Hermon was transported down and poured out on Mount Zion.*

This Psalms describes the anointing that saturated Aaron as precious, so we can assume that there is an unique anointing that manifests when we dwelling together in unity.

Dictionary.com describes *Precious* as:
1. Of high price or great value; very valuable or costly

2. Highly esteemed for some spiritual, nonmaterial, or moral quality
3. Dear; beloved
4. Affectedly or excessively delicate, refined, or nice:
5. Adored, cherished, treasures, idolized, invaluable

This anointing is unique and different from the anointing we carry in our own unique giftings and callings. That there are invaluable treasures in our ability to not just unify but dwell together in unity.

What makes this anointing unique and strategic?
Well we recognize that:
- It descends from the head which I believe represents God as the head of or lives and the head of the unity we are exuding
- It is poured on top of the anointing that we are already mantled with and resides in our midst
- It is a tangible covering prostrated upon us as a reward from God for remaining in a continual place of unity
- It is also a kingdom key as we read further that the Lord commanded the blessing — Life forevermore because of the dwelling of unity among the brethren

The word <u>Command in the Hebrew is *Sawa* and means:</u>
1. command, charge, give orders, lay charge, give charge to, order
2. To bid, commission, ordain, an ordination

WHEWWWW! When we dwell together in unity a commission of eternal blessings is released. As we continue in covenant, the precious oil continues to flow, and the ordained blessings continue to be released. WHEWWWW!

I believe Aaron was used as a comparison in this scripture because he had experienced the consequences of dwelling in disunity. In Exodus 32, we find Aaron assisting and directing the Israelites in making a golden calf.

> ***Exodus 32:1-5*** *- And when the people saw that Moses delayed to come down out of the mount, the people gathered themselves together unto Aaron, and said unto him, Up, make us gods, which shall go before us; for as for this Moses, the man that brought us up out of the land of Egypt, we wot not what is become of him. And Aaron said unto them, Break off the golden earrings, which are in the ears of your wives, of your sons, and of your daughters, and bring them unto me. And all the people brake off the golden earrings which were in their ears, and brought them unto Aaron. And he received them at their hand, and fashioned it with a graving tool, after he had made it a molten calf: and they said, these be thy gods, O Israel, which brought thee up out of the land of Egypt. And when Aaron saw it, he built an altar before it; and Aaron made proclamation, and said, tomorrow is a feast to the Lord.*
>
> ***Verse 17-19*** *- And when Joshua heard the noise of the people as they shouted, he said unto Moses, There is a noise of war in the camp. And he said, It is not the voice of them that shout for mastery,*

neither is it the voice of them that cry for being overcome: but the noise of them that sing do I hear.

- Joshua said that he didn't hear the shouts of mastery. The shouts of mastery would be the voices of the mighty ones that testify, proclaim, prophecy, call forth and release forth. He didn't hear these voices.
- Neither did they hear those who had been attacked or defeated by the enemy so this war wasn't from the devil or outsiders.
- What they heard was singing but the word sing in this passage of scripture is not the singing of praise and worship. This word "*sing*" is "*Ana*" and means depression, oppression, affliction, mishandle, downtrodden.
- It was a singing of demonic war of chaos and disunity resounding from within the camp.
- This is also the sound of self-sabotage as God had shown Himself mighty to the Israelites and though they had been delivered naturally from Egypt, spiritually they still held and operated in some of the mentalities of the old season...the old region....of being a slave of Egypt.

If you read this story in detail, you will find that the people became anxious and weary because Moses and Joshua went to meet with God and didn't come back in what they considered to be timely manner. They decided to make their own idol god to lead them and encouraged one of their major leaders Aaron to assist and direct them in making a golden calf. Aaron gave into disunity, division, and even broke covenant between God, Moses as the leader of Israel, and the people, and the results would be continual curses rather than blessings coming upon the people.

> ***Verse 25-27 The Amplified Bible*** - *And when Moses saw that the people were unruly and unrestrained (for Aaron had let them get out of control, so that they were a derision and object of shame among their enemies), Then Moses stood in the gate of the camp, and said, Whoever is on the Lord's side, let him come to me. And all the Levites [the priestly tribe] gathered together to him. And he said to them, Thus says the Lord God of Israel, Every man put his sword on his side and go in and out from gate to gate throughout the camp and slay every man his brother, and every man his companion, and every man his neighbor.*

> ***Verse 35 The Amplified Version*** - *And the Lord sent a plague upon the people because they made the calf which Aaron fashioned for them.*

When reading the entire chapter of Exodus 32, you will find Aaron blaming the people for his actions in making the golden calf. Though he gave direction of how to make it and actually formed it with his own hands, he acted as if the calf miraculously appeared out of the fire when Moses questioned him about it.

> ***Verse 2-5*** - *So Aaron replied, Take the gold rings from the ears of your wives, your sons, and daughters, and bring them to me. So all the people took the gold rings from their ears and brought them to Aaron. And he received the gold at their hand*

> *and fashioned it with a graving tool and made it a molten calf; and they said, these are your gods, O Israel, which brought you up out of the land of Egypt! And when Aaron saw the molten calf, he built an altar before it; and Aaron made proclamation, and said, tomorrow shall be a feast to the Lord.*
> **Verse 24 The Amplified Version** - *I said to them, Those who have any gold, let them take it off. So they gave it to me; then I cast it into the fire, and there came out this calf.*

From this scripture we can discern that the reason continual dwelling in unity is important, as when disunity occurs further sin manifests, causing greater division and greater defying of the covenant of unity. The more Aaron lied and gave excuses for his actions, the more he separated himself from the Israelites and from God.

When considering unity/the power of agreement among the arts:
- The vocal song expresses the breath of God
- The instruments expresses the heartbeat of God
- The dance expresses the movement of God
- The sound ministry expresses the frequency of God
- The artist expresses the creativity of God

Though each is a distinct atmospheric expression, they all serve the same purpose spiritually:
- All of these expressions have the power and authority to change any atmosphere and reclaim the land

- They all have the power to break demonic chains and put demons to flight
- They all can be used to war and intercede, and they all have the power to bring forth the breathtaking glory of God
- They all have the power to deliver, heal, save and to produce, miracles, signs and wonders

  1. Instruments release the sound of heaven on earth.
  2. Psalmist take the sound from instruments and harmonize the voice of God, while creating sounds that releases transformation
  3. The dancers interpret what has been demonstrated through the music and transformed through the song displaying the physical revelation and establishment of God
  4. The arts reveals a visible portrait of what God is speaking, doing and solidifying
  5. The sound ministry helps to further release, establish solidify God's work in the region and heavenlies

Instruments, songs, and dances serve as an atmospheric threefold cord, while art and the sound ministry becomes fortifying supports that further equips the arts as its own fivefold weapon that cannot be infiltrated.

> *Ecclesiastes 4:12* - *And if one prevails against him, two shall withstand him; and a threefold cord is not quickly broken.*

> ***Deuteronomy 32:30*** - *How should one chase a thousand, and two put ten thousand to flight, except their Rock had sold them, and the LORD had shut them up?*
>
> ***Leviticus 26:8*** - *Five of you will chase a hundred, and a hundred of you will chase ten thousand, and your enemies will fall by the sword before you.*
>
> ***Judges 7:22*** - *And the three hundred blew the trumpets, and the LORD set every man's sword against his fellow, even throughout all the host: and the host fled to Bethshittah in Zererath, and to the border of Abelmeholah, unto Tabbath.*

Often these ministries are their own compartment within the church. They practice separately, operate independently of one another, and usually the musician and praise team is seen and treated with higher importance than the other ministries. This is generally because music and singing has been widely accepted and seen as essential to the move of God, while the others have gone unexposed in their sufficiency. God however, has brought enlightenment in the other areas and has raised up ministers that can fulfill these duties with signs following. Thus such religious ranking tends to cause division, competition, and ostracism, while leaving an open door for the enemy to infiltrate when it is time for all to come together and work as one unified arsenal.

Some of the situations that occur because of this religious ranking are as followed:
- Leaders and members of the group competing for respect and thus not working together, or not willing to take direction from one another, even in instances where God is releasing strategy of greater glory and victory. Example, sound ministry not wanting to turn up the sound or fix the sound as by their standards it is already correct, yet the music or dance ministry feel otherwise.
- Leaders and members not having a clear revelation of the purpose of the other ministries, so they only deem their ministry valuable and want everyone to submit to their ministry customs and standards.
- Dance is not seen as a spiritual ministry and is often shunned in the church. Those that recognize that dance is of God, rarely support the ministry (even those among the arts), such to assist with changing the stronghold with the church body.

The challenge here is we tend to wait until ministry services to dwell together in unity. **We do not realize that praise and worship within itself is warfare.** Often, when praise and worship goes forth, it serves as some type of signal or alarm to the enemy that God's word, name, judgment and/or justice is about to be enforced.

Let us consider this theory using Psalms 150. The Hebrew word for *praise* in this scripture is *Haal* and one of its definitions is "*to flash forth light.*"

Usually when a light is flashing some type of signal is being released.
- Lights flashing on a car can be a signal of danger or the police are near.
- A flash of light going on and off could indicate a sign is distress.
- A flashlight going on and off could be an indication that the battery is low or the light is defected.
- Lightening flashing indicates a storm or judgment - a striking is occurring.

So if our praising is releasing flashes of light, then our praises are signaling or releasing an alarm that God's rule and will is being enforced in some fashion.

For this reason alone, the dwelling of unity is so essential. Our praise may be strong and boisterous, yet our signals are weak because of the open doors of disunity among the arts. The lack of hidden cohesiveness and segregation hinders us from being even more effective in seeing God answer prayers, release strategies, yield blessings, experiencing miracles, signs and wonders, having a consistent open heaven or effectively combating principalities, pulling down strongholds, and taking over territories.

We operate in measure rather than the fullness of the arts arsenal that is available to us, thus our results are a measure of victory and a measure of the pleasures of God's glory (*Psalms 16:11 You will show (sidebar comment: show is a revealing of spiritual light) me the path of life; In Your presence is fullness of joy; At Your right hand are pleasures forevermore*).

All throughout the bible we see the arts being used as an enforcement of warfare, God's word, name, judgment, justice, etc. And often the arts ministry is on the frontline of these contentions.

Unity of the Arts being used in Warfare:
Joshua's 6:3-5 - *You shall march around the city, all the men of war circling the city once. You shall do so for six days. Also seven priests shall carry seven trumpets of rams' horns before the ark; then on the seventh day you shall march around the city seven times, and the priests shall blow the trumpets. It shall be that when they make a long blast with the ram's horn, and when you hear the sound of the trumpet, all the people shall shout with a great shout; and the wall of the city will fall down flat, and the people will go up every man straight ahead.*

2Chronicles 20:20-25 - *And they rose early in the morning, and went forth into the wilderness of Tekoa: and as they went forth, Jehoshaphat stood and said, Hear me, O Judah, and ye inhabitants of Jerusalem; Believe in the Lord your God, so shall ye be established; believe his prophets, so shall ye prosper. And when he had consulted with the people, he appointed singers unto the Lord, and that should praise the beauty of holiness, as they went out before the army, and to say, Praise the Lord; for his mercy endureth for ever. And when they began to sing and to praise, the Lord set ambushments against the children of Ammon,*

Moab, and mount Seir, which were come against Judah; and they were smitten.

For the children of Ammon and Moab stood up against the inhabitants of mount Seir, utterly to slay and destroy them: and when they had made an end of the inhabitants of Seir, every one helped to destroy another. And when Judah came toward the watch tower in the wilderness, they looked unto the multitude, and, behold, they were dead bodies fallen to the earth, and none escaped. And when Jehoshaphat and his people came to take away the spoil of them, they found among them in abundance both riches with the dead bodies, and precious jewels, which they stripped off for themselves, more than they could carry away: and they were three days in gathering of the spoil, it was so much.

Arts Being Used the Declare God's Justice and Judgment:

Psalms 149 The Amplified Version - Praise the Lord! Sing to the Lord a new song, praise Him in the assembly of His saints! Let Israel rejoice in Him, their Maker; let Zion's children triumph and be joyful in their King! Let them praise His name in chorus and choir and with the [single or group] dance; let them sing praises to Him with the tambourine and lyre!

For the Lord takes pleasure in His people; He will beautify the humble with salvation and adorn the wretched with victory. Let the saints be joyful in the glory and beauty [which God confers upon them]; let them sing for joy upon their beds. Let the high praises of God be in their throats and a two-edged sword in their hands,

To wreak vengeance upon the nations and chastisement upon the peoples, to bind their kings with chains, and their nobles with fetters of iron, to execute upon them the judgment written. He [the Lord] is the honor of all His saints. Praise the Lord! (Hallelujah!)

Arts Being Used to Establish a Work God has Completed:

Exodus 15:18-21 *The Lord shall reign for ever and ever. For the horse of Pharaoh went in with his chariots and with his horsemen into the sea, and the Lord brought again the waters of the sea upon them; but the children of Israel went on dry land in the midst of the sea.*

And Miriam the prophetess, the sister of Aaron, took a timbrel in her hand; and all the women went out after her with timbrels and with dances. And Miriam answered them, Sing ye to the Lord, for he hath triumphed gloriously; the horse and his rider hath he thrown into the sea.

Ezra 3:10-11 *- And when the builders laid the foundation of the temple of the Lord, they set the priests in their apparel with trumpets, and the Levites the sons of Asaph with cymbals, to praise the Lord, after the ordinance of David king of Israel. And they sang together by course in praising and giving thanks unto the Lord; because he is good, for his mercy endureth for ever toward Israel. And all the people shouted with a great shout, when they praised the Lord, because the foundation of the house of the Lord was laid.*

Arts Flashing for Lights of Praise that Produce the Glory Cloud:

2Chronicles 5:13-14 - It came even to pass, as the trumpeters and singers were as one, to make one sound to be heard in praising and thanking the Lord; and when they lifted up their voice with the trumpets and cymbals and instruments of musick, and praised the Lord, saying, For he is good; for his mercy endureth for ever: that then the house was filled with a cloud, even the house of the Lord; So that the priests could not stand to minister by reason of the cloud: for the glory of the Lord had filled the house of God.

Arts Showing Forth the Goodness of God:
Psalms 92:1-5 - It is a good thing to give thanks unto the Lord, and to sing praises unto thy name, O most High: To shew forth thy lovingkindness in the morning, and thy faithfulness every night, Upon an instrument of ten strings, and upon the psaltery; upon the harp with a solemn sound. For thou, Lord, hast made me glad through thy work: I will triumph in the works of thy hands. O Lord, how great are thy works! And thy thoughts are very deep.

2Corinthians 10:3-6 - *For though we walk in the flesh, we do not war after the flesh: (For the weapons of our warfare are not carnal, but mighty through God to the pulling down of strong holds); Casting down imaginations, and every high thing that exalteth itself against the knowledge of God, and bringing into captivity every thought to the obedience of Christ; And having in a readiness to revenge all disobedience, when your obedience is fulfilled.*

<u>Weapon in the Greek is *Hoplon* and means:</u>
3. Utensil or tool (offensive for war)
4. Armor, an instrument
5. Any tool or implement for preparing a thing arms used in warfare
6. Arms used in warfare, weapons

<u>Warfare in the Greek is *Strateia* and means:</u>
2. Military service, i. e. (figuratively) the apostolic career (as one of hardship and danger): warfare
3. An expedition, campaign, military service, warfare
4. Paul likens his contest with the difficulties that oppose him in the discharge of his apostolic duties, as warfare

All through the bible we see how songs, sounds, dance and movement, praise, shouts, claps, are used in warfare. God uses the foolish things to confound the wise (*1Corinthians 1:27, Psalms 8:2*). Though He can use fleshly instruments, His weapons embody His spiritual nature and character. This means that the weapons God gives us, manifests from the spirit realm and from the reality and truth of who He is. Not from the world, our flesh, or our truth or perception. God's weapons manifest from His truth and His Spirit.

> ***John 4:24 The Message Version*** - *God is sheer being itself--Spirit. Those who worship him must do it out of their very being, their spirits, their true selves, in adoration.*

God's weapons are for the purposes of judging, destroying, demolishing, extinguishing, and dismantling strongholds, while conquering over the enemy.

God will use us and the very fashion of movement and expression of our existence as war club - a battle axe, to bring about His purpose and justice.

Whewwwww! Is anyone else getting excited and pumped up????

> **English Standard Version** - *You are my hammer and weapon of war: with you I break nations in pieces; with you I destroy kingdoms;*
>
> **The Message Version** - *God says, You, Babylon, are my hammer, my weapon of war. I'll use you to smash godless nations, use you to knock kingdoms to bits.*
>
> **KJV** - *Thou art my battle axe and weapons of war: for with thee will I break in pieces the nations, and with thee will I destroy kingdoms.*

I shared all those bible versions to vibrantly materialize this revelation into your spirit.

Battle axe in the Hebrew is *Mapes* and means *"a smiter, war club, club, a hammer."*

> **Isaiah 41:15-16** - *Behold, I will make thee a new sharp threshing instrument having teeth: thou shalt thresh the mountains, and beat them small, and shalt make the hills as chaff. Thou shalt fan them, and the wind shall carry them away, and the whirlwind shall scatter them: and thou shalt rejoice in the Lord, and shalt glory in the Holy One of Israel.*

Prophetically and even naturally, mountains are high places or positions and thoughts of pride and idol worship. God is saying I will transform you into a threshing sledge that has teeth and you will trample and tear down mountains (the high places that exalt against me). And then you will use your hand to fan (disperse, winnow) the mountains. Your fanning hand -winding arms, shall be like a wind, even a whirlwind - a hurricane that scatters the mountains for my glory. Whewwwwww!

Activation: Have everyone focus on one high place in the region. Declare that God has turned them into a threshing sledge. Then have them fan and wind their arms like a hurricane to displace the high place.

Even as God use us as weapons, He has a storehouse of artillery.

> *Jeremiah 50:25 New Living Translation - The LORD has opened his armory and brought out weapons to vent his fury. The terror that falls upon the Babylonians will be the work of the Sovereign LORD of Heaven's Armies.*
>
> **The Amplified Version** - *The Lord has opened His armory and has brought forth [the nations who unknowingly are] the weapons of His indignation and wrath, for the Lord God of hosts has work to do in the land of the Chaldeans.*
>
> **New English Translation** - *I have opened up the place where my weapons are stored. I have brought out the weapons for carrying out my wrath. For I,*

the Lord GOD who rules over all, have work to carry out in the land of Babylonia.

The Message Version Verse 25-26 - *I, God, opened my arsenal. I brought out my weapons of wrath. The Master, God –of–the–Angel–Armies, has a job to do in Babylon. Come at her from all sides! Break into her granaries! Shovel her into piles and burn her up. Leave nothing! Leave no one!*

I believe this storehouse - arsenal of artillery, resides in us through the Holy Spirit as well as in heaven.

Isaiah 13:2-5 The Amplified Version - *Raise up a signal banner upon the high and bare mountain, summon them [the Medes and Persians] with loud voice and beckoning hand that they may enter the gates of the [Babylonian] nobles. I Myself [says the Lord] have commanded My designated ones and have summoned My mighty men to execute My anger, even My proudly exulting ones [the Medes and Persians] – those who are made to triumph for My honor.*

Hark, the uproar of a multitude in the mountains, like that of a great people! The noise of the tumult of the kingdoms of the nations gathering together! The Lord of hosts is mustering the host for the battle. They come from a distant country, from the uttermost part of the heavens [the far east] – even the Lord and the weapons of His indignation – to seize and destroy the whole land.

God assembles His remnant that praise and worship Him, to accompany Him as He execute His plans against the enemy. God says they come from remoteness, distant lands, secret places and from heaven. The mighty remnant come as weapons of war to assist God in the battle.

> ***The Message Version Verse* 5** - *They come from far-off countries, they pour in across the horizon. It's God on the move with the weapons of his wrath, ready to destroy the whole country.*

We discern from this passage of scripture that it is so essential to grasp that we are the very embodied war club and arsenal of God, designed to crush the enemy, redeem people, and conquer the region. Lets' look at some other ways God use our bodies as war clubs

High praise in your mouth and a two edge sword in your hand:

> **Psalms 149:6-9** - Let the high praises of God be in their throats and a two-edged sword in their hands, to wreak vengeance upon the nations and chastisement upon the peoples, to bind their kings with chains, and their nobles with fetters of iron, to execute upon them the judgment written. He [the Lord], is the honor of all His saints. Praise the Lord! Hallelujah!

Praise in this scripture is *Halah* and means:
1. To shine, to shine (fig. of God's favor)
2. To flash forth light
3. To praise, boast, be boastful
4. Boastful ones, boasters (participle)
5. To boast, make a boast, glory, make one's boast
6. To be praised, be made praiseworthy, be commended, be worthy of praise
7. To make a fool of, make into a fool, to act madly, act like a madman

This is not just a praise, but a prophetic act of complete abandonment that declares who God is, yet also the very praise itself jails the enemy, assault his land, and executes the judgments and plans of the Lord among people and nations.

A high praise sets off an alarm while declaring the judgment of God.

High in the Hebrew is *Rowmĕmah* and means:
1. Uplifting, arising, to get up, rise
2. To originate from a source
3. To come into being or to attention

Whether speaking, declaring or praising God, we should be causing an uprising, sounding an alarm in someone or within the atmosphere.

The primitive root word of High is Ruwa *(Rua)* and means:

1. To mar (especially by breaking); figuratively, to split the ears (with sound)
2. Shout, (for alarm or joy), noise, alarm, cry, cry out, to shout for
3. Triumph, raise a sound, give a blast
4. To shout a war-cry or alarm of battle, to sound a signal for war or march
5. To shout in triumph (over enemies), to shout in applause, to shout (with religious impulse)
6. To cry out in distress, to utter a shout, a shout for joy, to shout in triumph, destroy

Ruwa is also same Hebrew word for the word "Shout" mentioned in Jeremiah 50:15 as a weapon against Babylon and Joshua 6 when the Israelites sought to possess the promise land.

> ***Jeremiah 50:15*** *- Shout against her on every side! She surrenders, her towers fall, her walls are torn down. Since this is the vengeance of the LORD, take vengeance on her; do to her as she has done to others.*

The Amplified Version - *Raise the battle cry against her round about! She gives her hand [in agreement] and surrenders; her supports and battlements fall, her walls are thrown down. For this is the vengeance of the Lord: take vengeance on her; as she has done [to others], do to her.*

The Message Version - *Shout battle cries from every direction. All the fight has gone out of her. Her defenses have been flattened, her walls smashed. Operation God's Vengeance. Pile on the vengeance! Do to her as she has done. Give her a good dose of her own medicine!*

Joshua 6:1-5 - *Now Jericho was straitly shut up because of the children of Israel: none went out, and none came in. And the LORD said unto Joshua, See, I have given into thine hand Jericho, and the king thereof, and the mighty men of valour. And ye shall compass the city, all ye men of war, and go round about the city once. Thus shalt thou do six days.*

And seven priests shall bear before the ark seven trumpets of rams' horns: and the seventh day ye shall compass the city seven times, and the priests shall blow with the trumpets. And it shall come to pass, that when they make a long blast with the ram's horn, and when ye hear the sound of the trumpet, all the people shall shout with a great shout; and the wall of the city shall fall down flat, and the people shall ascend up every man straight before him.

There are some people that will let out a yell or scream when they are angry or upset or stress. They think this releases tension but actually it increases it....it also sets off a signal. It sets off an alarm to those around the person that there is an even greater level of suppressed anger or stress that is waiting to explode.
I find this interesting because if we consider the high praise scripture, Jesus equipped us with this sound to trigger Him when His presence is needed in our lives against the enemy, yet we will yell at one another, and scream to the top of our lungs when we are upset...yell at games, but when we are told to shout in church, we become a church mouse.

We even get mad when the praise leader keep provoking us in praise....we lack the revelation of the power our high praise have against the enemy.

Activation: Loose God's judgment against the enemy concerning those threats against unity among the arts in this region by yelling a high praise of JESUS name all together.

Joshua 6 says that the Israelites compassed around Jericho in silence which means they marched around it without uttering a word.

The word *Compass* in the Hebrew is *Cabab* and means:
1. To turn, turn about or around or aside or back or towards, go about or around, surround, encircle

2. Change, to change direction, to march or walk around, go partly around, circle about, skirt, make a round, make a circuit, go about to, surround, encompass
3. Turn oneself, close round, turn round, to be turned over to, to transform, to encompass, surround, to come about, assemble round
4. To enclose, envelop, to reverse, bring over, turn into, bring round
5. To cause to go around, surround, encompass, to be turned, to surround

Activation: Have this demonstrated by calling up two people....have one be mean to the other. Have the silent person walk around the mean one without retaliating.

Silence baffles the enemy and creates curiosity that can torment the enemy with fear and dread.

And marching - Whewwwwww! Lets' look at what God says about our feet.
Demolition Feet

> *Deuteronomy 11:24 - Every place whereon the soles of your feet shall tread shall be yours: from the wilderness and Lebanon, from the river, the river Euphrates, even unto the uttermost sea shall your coast be.*

> *Deuteronomy 33:29 - Happy art thou, O Israel: who is like unto thee, O people saved by the LORD, the shield of thy help, and who is the sword of thy excellency! and thine enemies shall be found liars*

unto thee; and thou shalt tread upon their high places.

Joshua 1:3 - *Every place that the sole of your foot shall tread upon, that have I given unto you, as I said unto Moses.*

Psalms 91:13 - *Thou shalt tread upon the lion and adder: the young lion and the dragon shalt thou trample under feet.*

Psalms 108:13 - *Through God we shall do valiantly: for he it is that shall tread down our enemies.*

Malachi 4:3 - *And ye shall tread down the wicked; for they shall be ashes under the soles of your feet in the day that I shall do this, saith the LORD of hosts.*

Luke 10:19 - *Behold, I give unto you power to tread on serpents and scorpions, and over all the power of the enemy: and nothing shall by any means hurt you.*

Webster's definition of *Tread* as:
1. To trod, trodden, walk on, over, or along
2. To press beneath the feet; trample.
3. To subdue harshly or cruelly; crush.
4. To form by walking or trampling: tread a path.
5. To execute by walking or dancing: a manner
6. to crush or squash by or as if by treading
7. to subdue or repress, as by doing injury (to), to tread on one's inferiors

Our feet denotes freedom and mobility. They subdue territory while establishing kingly dominion. Feet solidify the generational inheritance that God has promised. They also snuff out and break curses off the land and reclaiming territory.

I decree that you are coming into the revelation that as you journey about life or dance in ministry, you trample over, crush, subdue, repress - the enemy.

Walking around Jericho was a prophetic act that manifested victory in seven days. The Israelites walked around in silence, blowing shofar and shouting at the command of the Lord and BAM...walls shattered.

Jericho was a gateway to where the Israelites were going. It also was a stronghold because there was no way to get to the promise land except the Israelites pass through Jericho. So, Jericho was the obstacle and even the principality that was standing between what God had said was theirs.

The Lord has had many great prophecies over your lives, family...your region...nation....what alarms are you releasing through your ministry to bring down these barriers so His kingdom can be established? Are you effectively utilizing your feet...your dance and even just your ability to walk in authority, to compass the enemy or has he encircled you?

Activation: Have the people stand up and march to activate this new revelation in their feet.

Switchblade Hands

Psalms 144 - *Blessed be the LORD my strength, which teacheth my hands to war, and my fingers to fight:*

Psalms 18:30-34 - *For by thee I have run through a troop; and by my God have I leaped over a wall. As for God, his way is perfect: It is God that girdeth me with strength, and maketh my way perfect. He maketh my feet like hinds' feet, and setteth me upon my high places. He teacheth my hands to war, so that a bow of steel is broken by mine arms.*

<u>Hands is Yad in the Hebrew:</u>
The word hands has a hosts of definitions but some of them are as followed:
1. Dominion, power, service,
2. draw with strength,
3. stroke, terror, ministry

One day the Lord revealed to me that our hands were like daggers. A dagger is a short, sword like weapon with a pointed blade used for stabbing - it is a switchblade!

So our hands are like powerful switchblades God uses as terrors against the enemy. And as God teach our hands to war, our switchblades become so spiritually strong that we can literally break bows of steel. WHEWWWW! BAMMMM Devil!

The Blasting Clap

Psalms 47:1-5 - *O clap your hands, all ye people; shout unto God with the voice of triumph. For the LORD most high is terrible; He is a great King over all the earth. He shall subdue the people under us, and the nations under our feet. He shall choose our inheritance for us, the excellency of Jacob whom He loved. Selah. God is gone up with a shout, the LORD with the sound of a trumpet.*

In this scripture *Clap* in the Hebrew is *Taqa* and means:
1. To blow, clap, strike, sound, thrust, give a blow, blast
2. To thrust, drive (of weapon)
3. To give a blast, give a blow
4. To strike or clap hands
5. To be blown, blast (of horn)
6. To strike or pledge oneself

You think you are just clapping but God says our claps strike - sends out blasts and blows.

When studying the shifting power of the clap in your personal time, you will find scriptures where the clap looses shame, contempt, anger, scorn, grief, judgment against the enemy *(Lamentations 2:15, Number 24:10, Nahum 3:19)*

EZEKIEL THE CLAPPING PROPHET

Ezekiel 21:14-15 - *Thou therefore, son of man, prophesy, and smite thine hands together, and let the sword be doubled the third time, the sword of the* *slain: it is the sword of the great men that are slain, which entereth into their privy chambers. I have set the point of the sword against all their gates, that [their] heart may faint, and [their] ruins be multiplied: ah! [it is] made bright, [it is] wrapped up for the slaughter.*

GOD ALMIGHTY CLAPPED

Ezekiel 21:16-17 - *Go thee one way or other, either on the right hand, or on the left, whithersoever thy face is set. I will also smite mine hands together, and I will cause my fury to rest: I the LORD have said it.*

<u>Smite</u> in these scriptures is <u>Nakah</u> and means:
1. To strike, smite, hit, beat, slay, kill
2. To be stricken or smitten
3. To beat, scourge, clap, applaud, give a thrust
4. To kill, slay (man or beast)
5. To attack, attack and destroy, conquer, subjugate, ravage
6. To chastise, send judgment upon, punish, destroy
7. To receive a blow, be wounded, beaten
8. To be (fatally) smitten, be killed, be slain
9. To be attacked and captured
10. To be smitten (with disease) to be blighted (of plants)

In these passages of scripture, we see God encouraging Ezekiel to clap and then God almighty promises to also release a clap. The reason God tells Ezekiel to clap is because He is releasing a sword of judgment against those in idolatry.

Activation: Have the people get in group of three or four. Place one person in the middle. Have the person share a stronghold in their life that needs judging. Have the remainder of the group prophecy, while clapping over the person.

Finger of God

> ***Luke 11:20-22 The Amplified Version*** *- But if I drive out the demons by the finger of God, then the kingdom of God has [already] come upon you. When the strong man, fully armed, [from his courtyard] guards his own dwelling, his belongings are undisturbed [his property is at peace and is secure]. But when one stronger than he attacks him and conquers him, he robs him of his whole armor on which he had relied and divides up and distributes all his goods as plunder (spoil).*

A *finger* is used to for the following:
1. To inform against or identify (a criminal) to the authorities:
2. To designate as a victim or offender.
3. To indicate exactly
4. A projector or pointer
5. Synonyms: antenna, claw, digit, extremity, feeler, hook, pinky, pointer, tactile member, tentacle

God revealed to me that when pointed, fingers are identifiers, judgers. They reveal and expose that which was once hidden, blended, or not judged.

We are not even talking about the power of the whole hand anymore, but just a finger. Now imagine what your whole hand does if your finger has this much power?

The word *Out* is *Ekballō* in the Greek and means:
1. To eject (literally or figuratively): — bring forth,
2. Cast (forth, out), drive (out), expel, leave,
3. Pluck (pull, take, thrust) out, put forth (out), send away (forth, out).
4. Cast out, cast bring forth, pull out, send forth
5. Send out, with notion of violence
6. Cast out of the world, be deprived of the power and influence he exercises in the world
7. To expel a person from a society: to banish from a family
8. To compel one to depart; to bid one depart, in stern though not violent language
9. To employed that the rapid motion of the one going is transferred to the one sending forth
   a. to command or cause one to depart in haste
10. To draw out with force, tear out, with implication of force overcoming opposite force
11. To cause a thing to move straight on its intended goal
12. To reject with contempt, to cast off or away

Dictionary.com defines *Cast* as:
1. A throw to the side
2. Synonyms: casting, ejection, expulsion, fling, flinging, heave, heaving, hurl, hurling, launching, lob, lobbing, pitch, pitching, projection, propulsion, shooting, sling, slinging, thrust, thrusting, toss, tossing

Activation: Have the people spread out and minister in movement to a warfare song, where all they are doing is using their finger against the enemy.

Though we tend to take these acts for granted, God views and uses them as powerful weapons that can bring forth great deliverance against the enemy.

Closing Activation: Decree that they have shifted into being the very embodiment of God, and are now God's war club artillery of mass destruction.

The Shifting Power of The Battering Ram

In this season of the body of Christ, there has been an increase of the shifting power of the "*battering ram.*"

Wikipedia Online Encyclopedia defines a *Battering Ram* as:
A battering ram is a siege engine originating in ancient times and designed to break open the masonry walls of fortifications or splinter their wooden gates. It was used, too, in ancient Roman mines and quarries to attack hard rocks. In its simplest form, a battering ram is just a large, heavy log carried by several people and propelled with force against an obstacle. The ram would be sufficient to damage the target if the log was massive enough and/or it were moved quickly enough, that is, if it had enough momentum.

You can usually recognize when a *battering ram* shifting is operating in a service because there is a repeating of a phrase or act where breakthrough or a sense of release in the spirit or natural realm is being pursued.

We observe the shifting power of battering through:

- Song and music as the praise and worship team, psalmist, or musician may repeat a phrase or play or strike a tune over and over.
- Praise dancers as the dance minister or team may dance in on spot or direction for a specific amount of time, minister the same move continuously, or minister a different move but strike

simultaneously to dislodge whatever is being battered against.
- Intercessor and warriors may repeat phrases or scriptures, decree continuously on a particular subject or combat continuously against a stronghold, sin, or situation.
- Preacher may have a congregation repeat a command or phrase over and over to break down barriers or stronghold in that area or the preacher may state a reoccurring theme or charge through his or her message to contend for breakthrough in the people or solidify the word in the people.
- Teachers, preachers, and ministers may have workshops or series on various topics to break bondages off of people so they can be free in particular areas of their lives.
- Prophets, apostles, etc., may give a prophecy, word of wisdom, revelation, understanding, knowledge, or counsel over and over or give them with similar themes to breakthrough obstacles of resistance, dullness or rebellion against the word
- A person may speak fiercely in tongues (in their prayer language) to batter in intercessor or warfare

<u>*Batter* in Merriam Webster's Online Dictionary means:</u>
1. To beat persistently or hard; pound repeatedly
2. To damage by beating or hard usage
3. To deal heavy, repeated blows; pound steadily
4. any of various devices for battering, crushing, driving, or forcing something, esp. a battering ram

5. A heavy beak or spur projecting from the bow of a warship for penetrating the hull of an enemy's ship
6. A warship so equipped, esp. one used primarily for ramming enemy vessels
7. The heavy weight that strikes the blow in a pile driver or the like
8. To strike with great force; dash violently against
9. To cram; stuff, to push firmly
10. To force (a charge) into a firearm, as with a ramrod

<u>Ram</u> in Merriam Webster's Online Dictionary means:
1. A piece of machinery that is used to hit or lift something else
2. Any of various guided pieces for exerting pressure or for driving or forcing something by impact, especially a battering ram
3. A warship with a heavy beak at the prow for piercing an enemy ship
4. The plunger of a hydrostatic press or force pump
5. The weight that strikes the blow in a pile driver
6. Synonyms: bang, bash, bump, collide, crash, impact, impinge, knock, ram, slam, smash, strike, swipe, thud
7. Related Words: bounce, carom, clunk, glance, rebound, ricochet, skim, skip; contact, land, touch; brush, graze, kiss, nudge, scrape, shave, sweep; bulldoze, jostle, muscle, press, push

WHEWWWWW!!! To those definitions. My favorite is *"a piece of machinery that is used to hit or lift something else, to crush, collide, cram crash."*

In the natural we do not like when we bump into someone, or crash or collide into something. We can be knocked down, badly hurt, require medical attention, or have to repair or replace whatever is damaged. When battering in the spirit realm, we are not seeking to just bump into something or collide with it where repairs or needed. The purposes of battering in the spirit is to totally annihilate and overthrow whatever is hindering us from having breakthrough in our lives and in our relationship with God.

> **Ezekiel 29:6** - *And he shall set engines of war against thy walls, and with his axes he shall break down thy towers.*
>
> **The Amplified Version** - *And he shall set his battering engines in shock against your walls, and with his axes he will break down your towers.*
>
> **New International Version** - *He will direct the blows of his battering rams against your walls and demolish your towers with his weapons.*

The bible refers to *battering rams* as *"engines of war."* WHEWWWW! For those who are being used as God's battering rams, you are going forth as war engines. War engines shock, blast and break down walls. You become God's literal mechanical tool that tortures and annihilate the enemy. The more you hit the devil, the more damage you do to him and his camp. WHEWWWWWWW!

In this passage of scripture, God was after the walls and towers of Tyrus (study Ezekiel 26). Walls provide protection, structure and closes something off from its adversaries or anything that could pose a challenge to it. Towers tend to be large castles, pulpit, elevated stages or high places. Walls and towers are built to last and withstand weather, people, traffic, wear and tear. These walls and towers are generally ancient or territorial strongholds as they are built to endure throughout the years and generations. In saying that, we discern that when we are serving as a battering ram, we are coming against strong forces that can take many blows before it folds – dismantles. It requires the constant battering to break through the sustaining fortress to which it was built. The battering realm however, is built to handle the impact of blasting through walls and towers and possess the shifting power to blast right on through them. In this age where stubbornness and rebellion are fortified walls and towers against the divine government of God, we need battering realms to bulldoze the enemy and crush him to pieces. Ask God to give you the shifting power of the battering ram. WHEWWWWW!

Kingdom Weaponry
Weapons of Song & The Tongue
By: Akeysha Headley

2Corinthians 10:3-5 - *For though we walk in the flesh, we do not war after the flesh: (For the weapons of our warfare are not carnal, but mighty through God to the pulling down of strongholds.) Casting down imaginations, and every high thing that exalteth itself against the knowledge of God, and bringing into captivity every thought to the obedience of Christ; and having in a readiness to revenge all disobedience, when your obedience is fulfilled.*

1st Revelation we must have is that there is an enemy in which our weapon of song is to be used on. The most dangerous enemy is one that is concealed. Let's look at a scenario: You are asked to meet a friend for dinner however when you get there they don't show up. When they do arrive they come running towards you with the idea to kill you. How in the world would you feel? We cannot be like that in the in the spirit realm. We must recognize that the devil is not our friend and he is a **real** enemy.

Our Spiritual Offensive Weapons
We have two different types of weapons. The one type of weapons is used to fight against the enemy with- **offensive weapons -** and the other type of weapons is used to protect us from the attacks of the enemy - **defensive weapons**.

We will start by looking at offensive weapons.

Our Tongues

Our tongue is an organ for which we use for speaking with. It is a very dangerous and deadly weapon that we have. We have control over it and how we used it. We must use it wisely and with great caution.

Proverbs 15:4 says, *"A wholesome tongue is a tree of life..."*

Proverbs 18:21 says, *"Death and life are in the power of the tongue..."*

Our tongue is a very powerful weapon that can be used to bring "life or death." We must really watch what we speak and sing over others and over ourselves. We want to use it to bring death to the enemy and all of his works. On the other hand, we want to use it to bring life to the things that are of the Lord.

> Explore an example of when you have opened your mouth to sing and you know that you were singing "life" over someone. How did that feel?

Isaiah 41:15 says, *"Behold, I will make thee a new sharp threshing instrument having teeth: thou shall thresh the mountains, and beat them small, and make the hills as chaff."*

A threshing instrument is a sharp pointed object. Our tongue is an object like that. The Lord said that with this instrument, we would destroy the mountains (obstacles) of the enemy. These mountains of the enemy are: "obstacles, doubt and unbelief."

So when we are using our tongue to sing we have the power to literally tear down mountains or obstacles that the devil has tried to place in our own lives and the people of God.

Our tongue is also symbolic of: "a sword or knife and a bow to shoot or launch things with."

Sword or Knife of the Tongue

Psalm 52:2 says, *"Thy tongue ... like a sharp razor..."*

Psalm 57:4 says, *"... Their tongue a sharp sword."*

In these verses of scripture, we see that our tongue is like a sharp sword or other cutting instrument. A sword is used for fighting with and it is used to inflict injury and even bring death.

A sword is like a knife. In the hands of a skillful doctor, the knife is used to remove things that are dead or unhealthy to us so that way healing can come. As you sing you are cutting off the things that are bringing death to people, cutting off past hurts, pains, disappointments. That's powerful!!!!!

Our Words - Arrows

Words are a powerful offensive weapon that we have in our spiritual arsenal. They can be used to bind and strike the enemy with. How many song writers do we have in here? The words that God gives you work together with the power of tongue to set the captives free!

The Word of Our Testimony

Have you ever heard someone say "That song is my testimony?"

Revelations 12:11 says, *"And they overcame him... by the word of their testimony..."*

When we testify about what the Lord has done for us, we overcome the enemy. **It breaks the chains of fear, doubt, and unbelief that Satan uses to keep others bound and it keeps them from receiving things from the Lord.** The enemy doesn't like it when we share with others about all the things that the Lord has done for us. This is even more so when you are singing your testimony. I know that sometimes sharing your testimony even in song puts you in a vulnerable place. Can someone share how they have pressed through that vulnerable feeling in ministering your testimony through song?

Testifying through songs gives glory to the Lord for what He has done and creates an atmosphere for the same or similar things to happen as well. For example, when you sing about a healing or miracle that you have received, it creates and brings back that same spiritual atmosphere for other to receive their healing or for them to receive their miracle that they need.

By testifying, it also releases your faith and it builds the faith of the people hearing about it. They will say to themselves "If the Lord did that for him, He will do it for me." Tye Tribbett (Same God)

The Blood and Name of Jesus

Revelations 12:11 says, "And they overcame him by the blood of the Lamb..."

1 John1:7 says, "... The blood of Jesus Christ his Son cleanseth (frees) us from all sin."

Hebrew 2:14 says, "... That through death He might destroy him that had the power of death, that is, the devil."

1 John 3:8 says, "... That He (Jesus) might destroy the works of the devil."

In all these verses of scripture tells us that it is by His precious blood that He has "cleansed us, set us free, and destroyed the devil and all his works."

Jesus' blood completely destroys the devil. As you sing about the blood of Jesus people are being deeply cleansed. You are washing their spirit and providing them with an avenue of purity in which leads them deeper in God. Now look what happens when you sing the **name of Jesus!**

Mark 16:17-18 says, (17) *"... In My Name shall they cast out devils; they shall speak with new tongues." (18) "They shall take up serpents; and if they drink any deadly thing, it shall not hurt them; they shall lay their hands on the sick, and they shall recover."*

Philippians 2:9-10 says, (9) *"Wherefore God also highly exalted Him, and given Him a name which is above every name." (10) "That at the name of Jesus every knee should bow, of things in heaven, and things in earth, and things under the earth."*

The enemy has to yield to the Almighty Name of Jesus. There is nothing that can stand up to that Name. Every time the enemy hears that Name, he trembles.

Some of the best times spent in praise and worship are when the song lyrics are simply the name of Jesus on repeat! It causes an immediate shift to occur, in which the longer you sing it, the higher and deeper you shift into the presence of God. All at the same time of beating the devil's head in!

The Holy Spirit

Remember the activation we did at the beginning of the class? You were exercising one of your weapons as a singer. I want to talk about this in depth because I don't think we utilize this weapon enough.

The Holy Spirit gives us the right words to speak (Mark 13:11). The Holy Spirit also empowers us (Acts 1:8). With the power of the Holy Spirit that is in us, on us, and has been given to us, we now can do His work for the Kingdom of God.

1 Corinthians 14:2 says, *"For he that speaketh in an unknown tongue speaketh not unto men, but unto God: for no man understandeth..."*

When you are singing in the spirit you are being empowered and built up. You should be able to feel a mounting up of authority and God stretching out in you as you sing in the spirit. You should be able to shift atmospheres as you sing in the Spirit because God is shifting those atmospheres through you!

Isaiah 59:19 says, *"...When the enemy comes in like a flood, the Spirit of the Lord shall lift up a standard against him.*

The Holy Spirit helps us fight against the enemy. He is always the greatest factor in all that we do for the Lord and He increases the odds in our favor in our fight against the enemy. He is ready and will help us if we ask Him to.

In Joshua 23:3 it says, *"...For the Lord your God is He that hath fought for you."*

Judges 14:19 & 15:14-15 says, (14:19) *"And the Spirit of the Lord came upon him (Samson), and he went down to Ashkelon, and slew thirty men of them..."*

(15:14) "...The Spirit of the Lord came mightily upon him..." (15:15) "And he found a new jawbone of an ass, and put forth his hand, and took it, and slew a thousand men therewith."

In these verses of scripture, the Holy Spirit came upon Samson and helped him to kill a great number of the enemy. This is not possible in our own strength but with Him all this are possible.

When we sing in the spirit it empowers to enemies much greater than trying to in our own natural language or strength. The Lord is making intercession for us and through as we sing in the spirit and spreads to His people. It makes fighting the devil so much easier because we are no longer the one doing the fighting....He is fighting for us!!!!!!

What happens when sing in the Spirit?
2. It releases the glory of God into the earth.
3. It changes the spiritual atmosphere around us.
4. It is the key to unlocking the power of God that is within us.
5. It brings us in unity with what the Lord is doing and with heaven.

6. That is why the Lord said "open thy mouth and I will fill it." - Psalm 81:10 He will fill it with the living water that is springing up from within us. - John 4:14

7. It breaks the power of the enemy to keep us quiet when we don't know what to speak or pray.

8. It is our secret code of talking to the Father that the enemy cannot understand. So he is confused and doesn't know what to do, to stop us or try to hinder us.

9. The Holy Spirit is there with us making intercession to the Father - Romans 8:26-27

10. We keep the commandment of the Lord - 1 Corinthians 14:15, 37

11. We build up ourselves - 1 Corinthians 14:4

12. We convey the wondrous acts of God - Acts 2:11b

13. We build up and increase our faith - Jude 20

14. We are offering up a perfect prayer to the Lord - Romans 8:16-17

15. We pray for things that is beyond our knowledge and comprehension - Romans 8:26

16. It causes us to line up our spirit with the Holy Spirit - Romans 8:16-17

17. Is a holy instrument given by the Lord for rest and refreshing to all believers - Isaiah 28:11-12

18. It causes our inner man to be strengthened - Ephesians 3:16

19. It is a sign to the world that we know Him - Mark 16:17; 1 Corinthians 14:22
20. We speak the wisdom of God in a mystery, that the Holy Spirit will reveal - 1 Corinthians 2:7; 14:2

Other Offensive Weapons

Agreement (Songs that Encourage Agreement)

In order for two or more people to do something together, there has to be an agreeing on which means that there is unity. The enemy knows this is a powerful weapon that we have and does not want us to use it.

Matthew 18:19-20 says, *(19) "Again, I say unto you, That if two of you shall agree on earth as touching any thing that they shall ask, it shall be done for them of My Father which is in heaven." (20) "For where two or three are gathered together in My Name, there am I in the midst of them."*

Faith (Songs of Faith)

Faith is a tremendous weapon that we have. Our faith in Him and in what He said breaks off the chains of doubt and unbelief of the enemy that he uses to attack us with.

Here are some things that faith does.

- It opens doors, of the impossible - Mark 9:23
- Faith is the connector to the power of God for seeing things happen in the natural

- It is the key to unlocking the power of God that is within us
- It can move mountains and obstacles that the enemy puts in front of us - Matthew 17:20; Mark 11:22-23
- Defeats the doubt and unbelief that the enemy fights us with - Ephesians 6:16
- We receive the promises of God by it - Hebrews 11:33
- Healings and miracles happen by it - Matthew 17:18-20; 21:21-22; Mark 9:23; 11:23-24

Our Spiritual Defensive Weapons

Just as we much as we need to weapons to attack the devil and his camp, we need weapons to keep the devil from "scoring" or attacking all together. These weapons serve to protect the people of God through singing.

Belt of Truth

A belt used to hold something together and it requires a certain amount of strength to do this. So we see that the belt represents strength and power.

Ephesians 6:14 says, "...*Having your loins girt about with truth...*"

The truth that it is talking about here is the truth of and in the **Word of God**, both written and spoken

(rhema & logos). Psalm 119:160 says, "Thy Word is true from the beginning..."

John 14:6 says, "...I am... the truth..."

In Jesus and in His Word we get and receive; His strength and power. This is a very important piece of our spiritual armor. We need this otherwise we would become weak and fall in the heat of the battle.

Activation: Singing The Word

Ask someone to give their favorite scripture. Then ask for another volunteer. Have the volunteer sing the scripture over the person that gave it! Discuss this activation. I truly believe that we will begin to see more of this evolve during praise and worship. There was a season where the Lord would have me carry my Bible while singing on the praise team and He would direct me to a verse and I would begin to sing it to myself.

The Blood of Jesus

The "blood of Jesus" is as much of defensive weapon as an offensive weapon.

Exodus 12:7, 13 says, (7) *"And they shall take of the blood, and strike (put) it on the two side posts and on the upper door post of the houses... (13) And the blood shall be to you for a token upon the houses where ye are: and when I see the blood, I will pass over you, and the plague shall not be upon you to destroy you..."*

In these verses, we see that the blood of Jesus is our token which means: "**sign, a distinguishing mark, banner, or warning**." This is like a "No Trespassing" sign to the enemy.

So as you sing there will be times where you will need to use the blood of Jesus as a banner over people.

These next defensive weapons are atmospheric weapons!

Wall of Fire/ Pillar of Fire

Zechariah 2:5 says, *"For I, saith the Lord, will be a wall of fire round about..."*

The Lord said that He will be a wall of fire that is around us and the enemy cannot get at us. He doesn't like the fire and he knows someday soon that hell is where he will be for all of eternity. As you are singing there will be times God will direct you sing about His fire. Fire much like the Blood of Jesus is use to protect and build a hedge around.

In 2 Kings 6, we see that Elisha had a mountain of horses and chariots of fire around him that was protecting him from the armies of the Syrians.

Exodus 13:21 says, "And the Lord went before them by day in a pillar of a cloud, to lead them the way; and by night in a pillar of fire, to give them light; to go by day and night."

Fire also produces light in which the Lord use brings light to us or our pathway to help us to see His direction and to reveal to us the plans of the enemy.

The last two are atmospheres of worship we create as singers….as worship is our main weapons.

Cloud of Glory

Isaiah 4:5 says, *"And the Lord will create upon every dwelling place of mount Zion, and upon her assemblies, a cloud and smoke…for upon all the glory shall be a defence (covering)."*

The "cloud of glory" is a defense for us. It is also a canopy and a covering to protect us. What a wonderful defensive weapon to have for our protection from the enemy.

Secret Place - Shadow of His Wings

There is no other place that we would rather be then in the refuge of our Lord. This is our safety zone from the attacks of the enemy.

Psalm 91:1, 4, 9-10 says, *"(1) He that dwelleth in the secret place of the most High shall abide under the shadow of the Almighty. (4) He shall cover thee with His feathers and under His wings shalt thou trust… (9) Because thou hast made the Lord, which is my refuge, even the most High, thy habitation; (10) There*

shall no evil befall thee, neither shall any plague come nigh thy dwelling."

Psalm 17:8 says, *"... Hide me under the shadow (as protection, defense) of Thy wings."*

Psalm 32:7 says, *"Thou art my hiding place; thou shalt preserve (keep) me from trouble..."*

The secret place, His feathers and the shadow of His wings are wonderful places of protection from all the attacks of the enemy. The enemy can never get to us in those places unless we remove ourselves from those places of the Lord's protection.

The Sound Of The Glory Minstrel

Music is armor the produces transforming shifting sounds:

> **2Chronicles 5:13-14** - *It came even to pass, as the trumpeters and singers were as one, to make one sound to be heard in praising and thanking the Lord; and when they lifted up their voice with the trumpets and cymbals and instruments of musick, and praised* **(halal act like a mad man)** *the Lord, saying, for he is good; for his mercy endureth for ever: that then the house was filled with a cloud, even the house of the Lord; So that the priests could not stand to minister by reason of the cloud: for the glory of the Lord had filled the house of God.*

<u>Instruments is *Kliy* in the Hebrew and means:</u>
1. Vessel, weapon, jewel, ware
2. Armor bearer, armor, furniture, utensil article,
3. Implement (of hunting or war) implement (of music)
4. Implement, tool (of labour)
5. Equipment, yoke (of oxen)

As musicians you able to govern the atmosphere through sound:

> **Psalms 67:3-7** - *Let the people praise thee, O God; let all the people praise thee. O let the nations be glad and sing for joy: for thou shalt judge the people righteously, and govern the nations upon*

earth. Selah. Let the people praise thee, O God; let all the people praise thee. Then shall the earth yield her increase; and God, even our own God, shall bless us. God shall bless us; and all the ends of the earth shall fear Him.

<u>Praise</u> in this scripture is *Yada* and means:
1. To use (hold out) the hand; physically, to throw (a stone, an arrow) at or away
2. Especially to revere or worship (with extended hands)
3. Intensively, to bemoan (by wringing the hands), cast (out), (make) confess, confession, praise, shoot, (give) thanks, thanksgiving
4. To cast, cast down, throw down
5. To confess, confess (the name of God)

<u>Judge</u> is *Sapat* in the Hebrew and means:
1. To judge, pronounce sentence (for or against), to vindicate or punish;
2. By extension, to govern; passively, to litigate (literally or figuratively):
3. Avenge, that condemn, contend, defend, execute (judgment), (be a) judge, judgment, needs, plead, reason, rule, defend, deliver,
4. Govern, vindicate, punish
5. To act as law- giver or judge or governor (of God, man)
6. To rule, govern, judge to decide controversy

The Amplified Version - *Let the peoples praise You [turn away from their idols] and give thanks to You, O God; let all the peoples praise and give thanks to You. O let the nations be glad and sing for joy, for you will judge the peoples fairly and guide, lead, or drive the nations upon earth. Selah [pause, and calmly think of that]! Let the peoples praise You [turn away from their idols] and give thanks to You, O God; let all the peoples praise and give thanks to You! The earth has yielded its harvest [in evidence of God's approval]; God, even our own God, will bless us. God will bless us, and all the ends of the earth shall reverently fear Him.*

The Message *-God! Let people thank and enjoy you. Let all people thank and enjoy you. Let all far-flung people become happy and shout their happiness because you judge them fair and square, you tend the far-flung peoples. God! Let people thank and enjoy you. Let all people thank and enjoy you. Earth, display your exuberance! You mark us with blessing, O God, our God. You mark us with blessing, O God. Earth's four corners-- honor Him!*

Sounds dismantle principalities and strongholds:

When sounds govern adequately, it causes principalities and strongholds to collapse. It dismantles the fortified strongholds of the enemy and exposes his kingdom.

> ***Joshua 6:20*** - *So the people shouted when the priests blew with the trumpets (as giving a clear sound): and it came to pass, when the people heard*

the sound of the trumpet, and the people shouted with a great shout, that the wall fell down flat, so that the people went up into the city, every man straight before him, and they took the city.

The Message Version *- The priests blew the trumpets. When the people heard the blast of the trumpets, they gave a thunderclap shout. The wall fell at once. The people rushed straight into the city and took it.*

<u>Blew is Taqa in the Hebrew and means:</u>
1. To clatter, slap (the hands together), clang (an instrument);
2. To drive (a nail or tent- pin, a dart, etc.)
3. To become bondsman by hand clasping, blow (a trumpet), cast, clap, fasten, pitch (tent), smite, sound, strike, thrust
4. To give a blow, blast, to thrust, drive (of weapon) to give a blast, give a blow to strike or clap hands
5. To be blown, blast (of horn), to strike or pledge oneself

When sound governs adequately it makes demons manifest and expose soulish issues:

***2Samuel 6:15-16** - So David and all the house of Israel brought up the ark of the Lord with shouting, and with the sound of the trumpet. And as the ark of the Lord came into the city of David, Michal Saul's daughter looked through a window, and saw King David leaping and dancing before the Lord; and she despised him in her heart.*

Sounds gathers the people in unity for war:

Nehemiah 4:19-20 The Amplified Version *- And I said to the nobles and officials and the rest of the people, the work is great and scattered, and we are separated on the wall, one far from another. In whatever place you hear the sound of the trumpet, rally to us there. Our God will fight for us.*

The Message Version *- Then I spoke to the nobles and officials and everyone else: "There's a lot of work going on and we are spread out all along the wall, separated from each other. When you hear the trumpet call, join us there; our God will fight for us."*

Psalms 47:5-7 *- God is gone up with a shout, the Lord with the sound of a trumpet. Sing praises to God, sing praises: sing praises unto our King, sing praises. For God is the King of all the earth: sing ye praises with understanding.*

Amplified Version *- God has ascended amid shouting, the Lord with the sound of a trumpet. Sing praises to God, sing praises! Sing praises to our King, sing praises! For God is the King of all the earth; sing praises in a skillful psalm and with understanding.*

The Message Version *- Loud cheers as God climbs the mountain, a ram's horn blast at the summit. Sing songs to God, sing out! Sing to our King, sing praise! He's Lord over earth, so sing your best songs to God.*

> *Aramaic Bible in Plain English* - *God went up in glory! Lord Jehovah with the sound of the trumpet!*

<u>Praises</u> in this scripture is *Zamar* and means:
1. The idea of striking with the fingers); properly
2. To touch the strings or parts of a musical instrument
3. Play upon it; to make music, accompanied by the voice
4. To celebrate in song and music, give praise, sing forth praises, psalms.

<u>Sound</u> in the Hebrew is *Qol* and means:
1. To call aloud; a voice or sound,
2. Sound aloud, bleating, crackling, cry (out),
3. Fame, lightness, lowing, noise, hold peace, (pro-) claim, proclamation,
4. Sing, sound, +spark, thunder, thundering, voice, yell

<u>Sound is atmospheric and it triggers the response of The Lord:</u>
The louder the sound, the greater God is exalted and the bigger he becomes. As he increases his judgment is released in our midst.

> ***Psalms 149:5-9*** - *Let the high **(romma which means exaltation, uplifting, arising)** praises of God be in their mouth, and a twoedged sword in their hand; To execute vengeance upon the heathen, and punishments upon the people; To*

bind their kings with chains, and their nobles with fetters of iron; To execute upon them the judgment written: this honour have all his saints. Praise ye the Lord.

Sounds raise the dead and has the ability to release a quick work for God: What could take years can occur in a twinkling of an eye with the correct sound. Spiritual sound thus dispels death and darkness and produce miracles. They shifts things from the corrupt and temporal to the eternal. Sounds shift us into the very nature and essence of our eternal God.

1Corinthians 15:52-54 *- In a moment, in the twinkling of an eye, at the last trump: for the trumpet shall sound, and the dead shall be raised incorruptible, and we shall be changed. For this corruptible must put on incorruption, and this mortal must put on immortality. So when this corruptible shall have put on incorruption, and this mortal shall have put on immortality, then shall be brought to pass the saying that is written, Death is swallowed up in victory. O death, where is thy sting? O grave, where is thy victory?*

Amplified Version *- In a moment, in the twinkling of an eye, at the [sound of the] last trumpet call. For a trumpet will sound, and the dead [in Christ] will be raised imperishable (free and immune from decay), and we shall be changed (transformed). For this perishable [part of us] must put on the imperishable [nature], and this mortal [part of us, this nature that is capable of* *dying] must put on immortality (freedom from death).*

And when this perishable puts on the imperishable and this that was capable of dying puts on freedom from death, then shall be fulfilled the Scripture that says, Death is swallowed up (utterly vanquished forever) in and unto victory. O death, where is your victory? O death, where is your sting?

The Message Version - *You hear a blast to end all blasts from a trumpet, and in the time that you look up and blink your eyes--it's over. On signal from that trumpet from heaven, the dead will be up and out of their graves, beyond the reach of death, never to die again. At the same moment and in the same way, we'll all be changed. In the resurrection scheme of things, this has to happen: everything perishable taken off the shelves and replaced by the imperishable, this mortal replaced by the immortal. Then the saying will come true: Death swallowed by triumphant Life! Who got the last word, oh, Death? Oh, Death, who's afraid of you now?*

God requires fresh and new songs and sounds:

Psalms 149:1-4 - *Praise ye the Lord. Sing unto the Lord a new song, and his praise in the congregation of saints. Let Israel rejoice in him that made him: let the children of Zion be joyful in their King. Let them praise his name in the dance: let them sing praises unto him with the timbrel* *and harp. For the Lord taketh pleasure in his people: he will beautify the meek with salvation.*

The Message Version - *Hallelujah! Sing to God a brand-new song, praise him in the company of all who love him. Let all Israel celebrate their Sovereign Creator, Zion's children exult in their King. Let them praise his name in dance; strike up the band and make great music! And why Because God delights in his people, festoons plain folk with salvation garlands!*

Often when the bible speaks of instruments, especially the trumpet, it speaks of giving a clear sound or a continuous sound as with the rams horn:

1Corinthians 7-8 - *And even things without life giving sound, whether pipe or harp, except they give a distinction in the sounds, how shall it be known what is piped or harped? For if the trumpet give an uncertain sound, who shall prepare himself to the battle?*

The Amplified Version - *If even inanimate musical instruments, such as the flute or the harp, do not give distinct notes, how will anyone [listening] know or understand what is played? And if the war bugle gives an uncertain (indistinct) call, who will prepare for battle?*

The Message Version - *If musical instruments— flutes, say, or harps—aren't played so that each*

> *note is distinct and in tune, how will anyone be able to catch the melody and enjoy the music? If the trumpet call can't be distinguished, will anyone show up for the battle?*

There is a strategic flow that is released in sound. This flow is necessary for moving in alignment with what God is desiring in a service.

> ***John 7:38 KJV*** *- He that believeth on me, as the scripture hath said, out of his belly shall flow rivers of living water.*

> **The Amplified Version** *- He who believes in Me [who cleaves to and trusts in and relies on Me] as the Scripture has said, From his innermost being shall flow [continuously] springs and rivers of living water.*

> **The Message Version** *- Rivers of living water will brim and spill out of the depths of anyone who believes in me this way, just as the Scripture says.*

<u>Flow</u> is <u>Rheo</u> in the Greek and means:
5. A prolonged form
6. Used to flow ("run"; as water), flow

<u>Rivers</u> is <u>Potamos</u> in the Greek and means:
7. A current, brook or freshet (as drinkable), i.e. running water
8. Flood, river, stream, water, a torrent

9. There is a prolong flow and even a current that praise and worship should flow on and it should shift us upward...upstream as we should constantly elevate if we are on the correct current with God.

Dictionary.com describes *Torrent* as:
10. A stream of water flowing with great rapidity and violence.
11. A rushing, violent, or abundant and unceasing stream of anything:
12. A violent downpour of rain.
13. A violent, tumultuous, or overwhelming flow:

This means as we are on the correct current, there should be an abundance of rivers flowing from our belly and even down pouring upon us from the heavenlies.

> *Psalms 46:4 - There is a river (prosperity, flood), the streams whereof shall make glad the city of God, the holy place of the tabernacles of the most High*

> *The NET Version - Verse 4-5 - A river brings joy to the city of our God, the sacred home of the Most High. God dwells in that city; it cannot be destroyed. From the very break of day, God will protect it.*

Waters usually represent the Holy Spirit, so this is a continuous flow of presence of God. Moreover water suggest a cleansing, refreshing, drenching.

<u>Waters</u> is Greek for *Hyáor* and means:
1. Waters in rivers
2. In fountains
3. In pools of the water
4. Of the deluge of water
5. In any of the earth's repositories
6. Of water as the primary element
7. Out of and through which the world that was before the deluge, arose and was compacted of the waves of the sea fig. used of many peoples

When waters flow things get swallowed up and drowned out. The fountains and the pools come to wash us from the old and make us new, wash us from the demonic and make us like God, refresh and empower us all the more in God.

>**Genesis 2:20** - *A river watering the garden flowed from Eden; from there it was separated into four headwaters.*
>
>**Psalms 16:11** - *You make known to me the path of life; you will fill me with joy in your presence, with eternal pleasures at your right hand.*
>
>**Psalms 23:2** - *He makes me lie down in green pastures, he leads me beside quiet waters,*
>
>**Psalms 36:8** - *They feast on the abundance of your house; you give them drink from your river of delights.*

> ***Psalms 43:3 -*** *Send me your light and your faithful care, let them lead me; let them bring me to your holy mountain, to the place where you dwell.*

If a person truly desire to operate in the shifting sounds of a minstrel, it is very important to live a sanctified and holy life and be set a part for God.

The word "minstrel" in the Hebrew is *"nagan"* and means to *"to play or strike strings, sing to the stringed instruments, melody, player, to make music, beat the tune with the fingers."* From this definition alone we discern that the anointing on a minstrel is one of warfare and using his or her giftings to strike blows against the enemy and his camp. Having open doors through unrepentant and blatant sin, only adds to the warfare and gives the enemy legal right to triumph and conquer over the minstrel. The minstrel must know that they are sound carriers, so whatever they subject themselves to, is what flows and filters through the sounds he or she produces and releases. This is one of the reasons people are being emotionally stimulated but not truly transformed during church and ministry services. Often times, sound in praise and worship is contaminated by what the minstrel has subjected themselves to outside of God's presence and will, so the sound released is not effective enough to shift and change someone's life. We may experience one or two miracles out of grace but the full anointing of the Holy Spirit is not flowing in purity so God cannot really operate in our contaminated midst. Churches and ministries have to not only govern the ministry but make minstrels accountable to the gifting and calling on their lives. The minstrel's lifestyle must be conducive to the nature and character of God so that God's sound can be produced with miracles, signs, and wonders.

David is our greatest example of a minstrel sold out for God. God described him as a man after His own heart and one who followed His commandments. Because David had a heart for God, he produced anointed and skillful sounds that brought deliverance even to his enemies, shifted atmospheres and gave him favor with people and with God.

> ***1Samuel 13-14*** - *But now thy kingdom shall not continue: the LORD hath sought him a man after his own heart, and the LORD hath commanded him to be captain over his people, because thou hast not kept that which the LORD commanded thee.*
>
> ***Acts 13:22*** - *After removing Saul, he made David their king. God testified concerning him: 'I have found David son of Jesse, a man after my own heart; he will do everything I want him to do.'*
>
> ***1Samuel 16:22*** - *And it came to pass, when the evil spirit from God was upon Saul, that David took an harp, and played with his hand: so Saul was refreshed, and was well, and the evil spirit departed from him.*
>
> ***1Samuel 18:7*** - *And the women answered one another as they played, and said, Saul hath slain his thousands, and David his ten thousands.*

David was prophetic and apostolic. David prophesied regarding Jesus Christ *(Psalm 22:16; Psalm 16:10; Isaiah 53:10-11; Psalm 68:18; Psalm 110:1)*
We also know of bible stories of how he consistently prophesied and established God's kingdom through praise, song, dance, war, declaration and music. The bible also reveals David's apostolic ability to shift and transform himself, people, and atmospheres through his minstrel anointing.

Recommended studies for the minstrel that truly desires to shift and transform lives and regions for Jesus:

Bishop Jackie Green's books can be purchased at JGMenternational.org:
- Worship Makers
- The Extraordinary Worshipper
- Throne Room Conduct
- Musician Makeover

Niles Bess' book and teaching CD's can be purchased at Amazon.com and Nilesbess.webs.com:
- Minstrels and Psalmists: The Key to Davidic Praise and Worship

The Glory Roar

A lot of spiritual experiences we equate or call roaring is really not roaring. **When God releases or requires a roar, or when someone is to lead a roar, it is a shifting signal that a judgment is being released. This judgment can bring war, deliverance, redemption (freedom), or consequences.** God determines when the roar should be loosed, and how the roar impacts a people or region once it is released. If judgment is not being released, you are not discharging a Godly roar. Other possibilities could be that you are birthing, interceding, or being personally delivered from a stronghold or bondage.

When God releases or requires a roar it is to perform one of the following:
- To war against His enemies or those that have bound His people
- To judge a sinful people or nation
- To judge evil or godless people and/or devils
- To respond to the roar of His people

The earth and even the world roars, but we are not to be moved by this roar.

> **Psalms 46:1-5** - *God is our refuge and strength, a very present help in trouble. Therefore will not we fear, though the earth be removed, and though the mountains be carried into the midst of the sea; Though the waters thereof roar and be troubled, though the mountains shake with the swelling thereof. Selah. There is a river, the streams*

> whereof shall make glad the city of God, the holy place of the tabernacles of the most High. God is in the midst of her; she shall not be moved: God shall help her, and that right early.
>
> **The Message Version** - *God is a safe place to hide, ready to help when we need him. We stand fearless at the cliff–edge of doom, courageous in seastorm and earthquake, before the rush and roar of oceans, the tremors that shift mountains. Jacob–wrestling God fights for us, God of angel armies protects us. River fountains splash joy, cooling God's city, this sacred haunt of the Most High. God lives here, the streets are safe, God at your service from crack of dawn.*

At times, the devil will roar and release war and a battle cry right in the midst of God's people - right in the midst of a service or church.

> **Psalms 74:4 The Amplified Version** - *In the midst of Your Holy Place Your enemies have roared [with their battle cry]; they set up their own [idol] emblems for signs [of victory].*

As God's people, we do not let the enemy draw us into a war by roaring. We do not respond to his war cry. We stay focus on worshipping God and harken to His voice only and His roar only.

> **Psalms 75:1-3 The Amplified Version** – *We give praise and thanks to You, O God, we praise and give thanks; Your wondrous works declare that Your Name is near and they who invoke Your*

Name rehearse Your wonders. When the proper time has come [for executing My judgments], I will judge uprightly [says the Lord]. When the earth totters, and all the inhabitants of it, it is I Who will poise and keep steady its pillars. Selah [pause, and calmly think of that]!

John 10:4-5 - And when he putteth forth his own sheep, he goeth before them, and the sheep follow him: for they know his voice. And a stranger will they not follow, but will flee from him:for they know not the voice of strangers.

Verse 27-28
My sheep hear my voice, and I know them, and they follow me: And I give unto them eternal life; and they shall never perish, neither shall any man pluck them out of my hand.

Voice is the Greek is *Phone* and means:
 1. Through the idea of disclosure; a tone (articulate, bestial or artificial),
 2. An address (for any purpose), saying or language
 3. Noise, sound, voice, be noised abroad
 4. A tone of inanimate things, as musical instruments
 5. A voice of the sound of uttered words speech of a language, tongue

Ohhhhh! Do you know who is calling you? Do you know the tone of your God's voice?

Spiritual and natural lions roar but it is God that feed them. We feast from God's hand as we roar out to Him. The *roar* in this next passage is *Saag* in the Hebrew and means, *"to rumble, be mighty, a conqueror."*

> **Psalms 104:21-23 The Amplified Version** - *You [O Lord] make darkness and it becomes night, in which creeps forth every wild beast of the forest. The young lions roar after their prey and seek their food from God. Man goes forth to his work and remains at his task until evening.*
>
> **The Message Version** - *When it's dark and night takes over, all the forest creatures come out. The young lions roar for their prey, clamoring to God for their supper. When the sun comes up, they vanish, lazily stretched out in their dens.*

God raises up a people, a remnant, to roar - roar out his judgment.

> **Isaiah 5:26-30 The Amplified Version** - *And He will lift up a signal to call together a hostile people from afar [to execute His judgment on Judea], and will hiss for them from the end of the earth [as bees are hissed from their hives], and behold, they shall come with speed, swiftly! None is weary or stumbles among them, none slumbers or sleeps; nor is the girdle of their loins loosed or the latchet (thong) of their shoes broken; their arrows are sharp, and all their bows bent; their horses' hoofs seem like flint, and their wheels like a whirlwind.*

Their roaring is like that of a lioness, they roar like young lions; they growl and seize their prey and carry it safely away, and there is none to deliver it. And in that day they [the army from afar] shall roar against [the Jews] like the roaring of the sea. And if one looks to the land, behold, there is darkness and distress; and the light [itself] will be darkened by the clouds of it.

The Message Version - *He raises a flag, signaling a distant nation, whistles for people at the ends of the earth. And here they come--on the run! None drag their feet, no one stumbles, no one sleeps or dawdles. Shirts are on and pants buckled, every boot is spit-polished and tied. Their arrows are sharp, bows strung, the hooves of their horses shod, chariot wheels greased.*

Roaring like a pride of lions, the full-throated roars of young lions,
They growl and seize their prey, dragging it off-- no rescue for that one! They'll roar and roar and roar on that Day, like the roar of ocean billows. Look as long and hard as you like at that land, you'll see nothing but darkness and trouble. Every light in the sky will be blacked out by the clouds.

GOD ROARS! Ohhhhhh HOW HE ROARS!

Isaiah 42:11-14 - *Let the wilderness and the cities thereof lift up their voice, the villages that Kedar doth inhabit: let the inhabitants of the rock sing, let them shout from the top of the mountains. Let* *them give glory unto the Lord, and declare his praise in the islands.*

The Lord shall go forth as a mighty man, he shall stir up jealousy like a man of war: he shall cry, yea, roar; he shall prevail against his enemies. I have long time holden my peace; I have been still, and refrained myself: now will I cry like a travailing woman; I will destroy and devour at once.

The Amplified Version - *Let the wilderness and its cities lift up their voices, the villages that Kedar inhabits. Let the inhabitants of the rock [Sela or Petra] sing; let them shout from the tops of the mountains! Let them give glory to the Lord and declare His praise in the islands and coastal regions.*

The Lord will go forth like a mighty man, He will rouse up His zealous indignation and vengeance like a warrior; He will cry, yes, He will shout aloud, He will do mightily against His enemies. [Thus says the Lord] I have for a long time held my peace, I have been still and restrained Myself. Now I will cry out like a woman in travail, I will gasp and pant together.

The Message Version - *Let the desert and its camps raise a tune, calling the Kedar nomads to join in. Let the villagers in Sela round up a choir and perform from the tops of the mountains. Make God's glory resound; echo his praises from coast to coast.*

God steps out like he means business. You can see he's primed for action. He shouts, announcing his arrival; he takes charge and his enemies fall into line: "I've been quiet long enough. I've held back, biting my tongue. But now I'm letting loose, letting go, like a woman who's having a baby--

We can roar for judgment and deliverance:

Isaiah 59:11 - *We roar all like bears, and mourn sore like doves: we look for judgment, but there is none; for salvation, but it is far off from us.*

The Amplified Version - *We all groan and growl like bears and moan plaintively like doves. We look for justice, but there is none; for salvation, but it is far from us.*

God responds to our roar:

Isaiah 59:16-17 The Message Version - *He couldn't believe what he saw: not a soul around to correct this awful situation. So he did it himself, took on the work of Salvation, fueled by his own Righteousness. He dressed in Righteousness, put it on like a suit of armor, with Salvation on his head like a helmet, Put on Judgment like an overcoat, and threw a cloak of Passion across his shoulders.*

The Amplified Version - *And He saw that there was no man and wondered that there was no intercessor [no one to intervene on behalf of truth and right]; therefore His own arm brought Him victory, and His own righteousness [having the Spirit without measure] sustained Him.*

> *For [the Lord] put on righteousness as a breastplate or coat of mail, and salvation as a helmet upon His head; He put on garments of vengeance for clothing and was clad with zeal [and furious divine jealousy] as a cloak.*

When God responds the roar, He comes to redeem and re-establish covenant with His people.

> **Isaiah 59:19-21** - *So shall they fear the name of the Lord from the west, and his glory from the rising of the sun. When the enemy shall come in like a flood, the Spirit of the Lord shall lift up a standard against him. And the Redeemer shall come to Zion, and unto them that turn from transgression in Jacob, saith the Lord.*
>
> *As for me, this is my covenant with them, saith the Lord; My spirit that is upon thee, and my words which I have put in thy mouth, shall not depart out of thy mouth, nor out of the mouth of thy seed, nor out of the mouth of thy seed's seed, saith the Lord, from henceforth and forever.*
>
> **The Amplified Version** - *So [as the result of the Messiah's intervention] they shall [reverently] fear the name of the Lord from the west, and His glory from the rising of the sun. When the enemy shall come in like a flood, the Spirit of the Lord will lift up a standard against him and put him to flight [for He will come like a rushing stream which the breath of the Lord drives]. He shall come as a*

> Redeemer to Zion and to those in Jacob (Israel) who turn from transgression, says the Lord.
>
> As for Me, this is My covenant or league with them, says the Lord:My Spirit, Who is upon you [and Who writes the law of God inwardly on the heart], and My words which I have put in your mouth shall not depart out of your mouth, or out of the mouths of your [true, spiritual] children, or out of the mouths of your children's children, says the Lord, from henceforth and forever.

God's desire it to redeem but if there is no turning, He will release the sword of His roar.

> ***Jeremiah 25:15-17*** *- For thus saith the Lord God of Israel unto me; Take the wine cup of this fury at my hand, and cause all the nations, to whom I send thee, to drink it. And they shall drink, and be moved, and be mad, because of the sword that I will send among them. Then took I the cup at the Lord 's hand, and made all the nations to drink, unto whom the Lord had sent me:*
>
> ***Verse 27*** *- Therefore thou shalt say unto them, Thus saith the Lord of hosts, the God of Israel; Drink ye, and be drunken, and spue, and fall, and rise no more, because of the sword which I will send among you.*
>
> ***Verse 30-31*** *- Therefore prophesy thou against them all these words, and say unto them, The Lord shall roar from on high, and utter his voice from his holy habitation; he shall mightily roar upon his*

habitation; he shall give a shout, as they that tread the grapes, against all the inhabitants of the earth. A noise shall come even to the ends of the earth; for the Lord hath a controversy with the nations, he will plead with all flesh; he will give them that are wicked to the sword, saith the Lord.

<u>Roar</u> in the Hebrew is *<u>Hama and means:</u>*
1. To make a loud sound, to be in great commotion or tumult,
2. Roar, noise, disquieted, sound, troubled, aloud, loud, clamorous
3. Concourse, mourning, moved, raged, raging, tumult, tumultuous, uproar
4. To murmur, growl, roar, cry aloud, mourn, rage, sound, make noise, tumult, be clamorous, be disquieted, be loud, be moved, be troubled, be in an uproar
5. To growl to murmur (fig. of a soul in prayer), to roar to be in a stir
6. Be in a commotion to be boisterous, be turbulent

<u>Dictionary.com defines *Roar* as:</u>
1. To utter a loud, deep cry or howl, as in excitement, distress, or anger.
2. To laugh loudly or boisterously
3. To make a loud sound or din, as thunder, cannon, waves, or wind
4. To function or move with a loud, deep sound, as a vehicle
5. To make a loud noise in breathing

Difference between a *roar* and a *travail*:
Travails are birthed for the purpose of life. A roar births for the purpose of death. Casualties in some form or fashion occur when a roar manifests. God is seeking to kill something that is hindering Him from fully being God in our midst. God is in pursuit of a prey. Though a roar can feel like, look, and sound like a travail, what comes forth is actually a sword (judging sound) that is released to devour something - devour sin, curses, people, devils, material things, ungodly things, etc.

> **Amos 3:4** - *Will a lion roar in the forest, when he hath no prey? Will a young lion cry out of his den, if he have taken nothing?*

> **The Message Version** - *Does a lion roar in the forest if there's no carcass to devour? Does a young lion growl with pleasure if he hasn't caught his supper?*

There is a remnant with the anointing to roar. This is biblical (refer to the scriptures above). Often when they roar, we do not stop the service to judge the sound or to hear what God is saying and releasing. We recognize that the sound is unique but we equate it to excitement, pointless yelling, demonic, travailing, or we just have not given it much thought at all. This is a challenge as truth is when that sound is released, God is releasing a judgment of some fashion either to us personally, as a congregation or to the region. Whoahhhhhh unto us if we are not discerning of God speaking to us in this fashion. We could very well be needing to repent and turn so God can release redemption or deliverance. We may need to enter into the roar with God as His ambassadors and war clubs. God could be advancing the kingdom among us and in us, taking over the region or releasing us into greater dimensions of His glory and kingdom and we fail to recognize it.

As I am writing this, God is revealing countless instances where I have personally and congregationally overlooked or misjudged His roar. Oh God forgive me/us, give me/us another chance to recapture those moments, and convicted me/us to be more discerning of your call. Shaking my head at myself.

> *Amos 3:6-8* - *Shall a trumpet be blown in the city, and the people not be afraid? Shall there be evil in a city, and the Lord hath not done it? Surely the Lord God will do nothing, but he revealeth his secret unto his servants the prophets. The lion hath roared, who will not fear? The Lord God hath spoken, who can but prophesy?*

> *The Message Version* - *When the alarm goes off in the city, aren't people alarmed? And when disaster strikes the city, doesn't God stand behind it? The fact is, God, the Master, does nothing without first telling his prophets the whole story. The lion has roared--who isn't frightened? God has spoken--what prophet can keep quiet?*

As we seek to operate in shifting power, it is important to humble ourselves unto God so we can distinguish His roar from that of the enemy.

> **1Peter 5:6-8** - *Humble yourselves therefore under the mighty hand of God, that he may exalt you in due time: Casting all your care upon him; for he careth for you. Be sober, be vigilant; because your adversary the devil, as a roaring lion, walketh about, seeking whom he may devour.*
>
> **The Amplified Version** - *Wherefore humble yourselves [demote, lower yourselves in your own estimation] under the mighty hand of God, that in due time He may exalt you, casting the [c]whole of your care [all your anxieties, all your worries, all your concerns, [d]once and for all] on Him, for He cares for you affectionately and cares about you [e]watchfully. Be well balanced (temperate, sober of mind), be vigilant and cautious at all times; for that enemy of yours, the devil, roams around like a lion roaring [[f]in fierce hunger], seeking someone to seize upon and devour.*

An *adversary* is an opponent or enemy that is against us. The Hebrew definition describes an *adversary* as an opponent in a suit of law, one that has a lawsuit against us. The lawsuit however, is illegal as we know that our case against the enemy was won through the cross and resurrection of Jesus. Therefore, Satan can roar, however, his sounds are only effective if we harken unto them. The devil roars in effort to draw us into a fight that distracts us from the sound and leading of God so he can devour, destroy and swallow us whole. This is the reason the scripture tells us to be humble, sober (calm, temperament) and vigilant (strict attention, watchful).

These attributes enable us to discern properly and know when God is roaring or when he enemy is blaring his counterfeit roar against us. We can discern the enemy's roar because it will lack the character and nature of God. Even when God is judging and warning, He operates from a well of reconciliation and restoration and generally leaves a pathway for us to repent and turn unto Him. The devil is always seeking to kill, steal, and destroy us. If he does provide a pathway, it usually requires a sacrifice unto Him or of ourselves, family, friends, generations, birthright, dignity, compromise, settling, and/or relationship with the God. It also generally requires us to come on his turf and terms while relinquishing the protection and covering of God. This is the reason the word says the devil roams - walks about - prowls. He is not under any authority or covering. He is submitted to no one and his judgment is already eternal damnation. When the devil roars, it is only out of his own anguish and pride to devour you the way he will be devoured on judgment day. Stay submitted to God. Resist the screeching roars of the devil and he will flee (*James 4:7*).

Rend The Heavens
A Shift Of Revival & Reconciliation

Isaiah 64:1-3 The Amplified Version - *Oh, that You would rend the heavens and that You would come down, that the mountains might quake and flow down at Your presence — As when fire kindles the brushwood and the fire causes the waters to boil — to make Your name known to Your adversaries, that the nations may tremble at Your presence! When You did terrible things which we did not expect, You came down; the mountains quaked at Your presence.*

The Message Version - *Oh, that you would rip open the heavens and descend, make the mountains shudder at your presence--As when a forest catches fire, as when fire makes a pot to boil--To shock your enemies into facing you, make the nations shake in their boots! You did terrible things we never expected, descended and made the mountains shudder at your presence.*

Merriam Webster's definition of *Shudder* is "*to tremble with a sudden convulsive movement, as from horror, fear, or cold.*"

Ecclesiastes 3:7. The Message Version - *A right time to rip out and another to mend, a right time to shut up and another to speak up*

The Amplified Version - *A time to rend and a time to sew, a time to keep silence and a time to speak*

<u>Rend is *Qara* in the Hebrew and means to;</u>
1. To cut, to cut out, to tear into pieces
2. To tear, rend to tear away or out to tear, rend asunder
3. To make wide or large (of eyes), to rend open (of heavens) to tear,
4. Rend (of wild beasts), to be rent, be split asunder
5. To separate into parts with force or violence: The storm rent the ship to pieces.

<u>Definition of *Rend* from Dictionary.com</u>
1. To tear apart, split, or divide
2. To pull or tear violently (often followed by away, off, up, etc.)
3. To tear (one's garments or hair) in grief, rage, etc.
4. To disturb (the air) sharply with loud noise
5. To harrow or distress (the heart) with painful feelings

Purpose of Rending:
- Make God's name known to His adversaries
- That the nations might tremble at God's presence
- To see God do impossible miracles that we do not expect or even know were necessary.
- To watch God move on our behalf
- To have God meet with us the righteous
- To deliver and cleanse sin and generational iniquity in God's people and the land

- To be delivered and healed of personal and generational afflictions and curses
- To be delivered from demonic oppressions
- To be delivered from captivity within the region where principalities have taken the land captive due to sin and God's people not properly governing the land
- To restore the fellowship broken due to sin
- To reconnect with God in a more powerful way that aligns us with destiny

> **Verse 5-8** Amplified Version - *You meet and spare him who joyfully works righteousness (uprightness and justice), [earnestly] remembering You in Your ways. Behold, You were angry, for we sinned; we have long continued in our sins [prolonging Your anger]. And shall we be saved?*
>
> *For we have all become like one who is unclean [ceremonially, like a leper], and all our righteousness (our best deeds of rightness and justice) is like filthy rags or a polluted garment; we all fade like a leaf, and our iniquities, like the wind, take us away [far from God's favor, hurrying us toward destruction].*
> *And no one calls on Your name and awakens and bestirs himself to take and keep hold of You; for You have hidden Your face from us and have delivered us into the [consuming] power of our iniquities.*
> *Yet, O Lord, You are our Father; we are the clay, and You our Potter, and we all are the work of Your hand.*

Rending is a supernatural act and request for deliverance by God's people. The people recognize that they have angered God and He has allowed them to reap the consequences of their sins. The people are now willing to be judged by God and acknowledge their sins so that God can visit the region and people with revival and restore His kingdom and will in their sphere of influence.

> ***2Chronicles 7:14*** - *If my people, which are called by my name, shall humble themselves, and pray, and seek my face, and turn from their wicked ways; then will I hear from heaven, and will forgive their sin, and will heal their land.*
>
> ***Isaiah 38:12*** - *Considering these [calamities], will You restrain Yourself, O Lord [and not come to our aid]? Will You keep silent and not command our deliverance but humble and afflict us exceedingly?*
>
> ***The Message Version*** - *In the face of all this, are you going to sit there unmoved, God? Aren't you going to say something? Haven't you made us miserable long enough?*

Rending is essential for the purposes of shifting one's self and the land back into alignment of God, where destiny can God forth according to His original plan for those people and that region.

Rending is a ripping away or off the sin nature and death iniquity. It will not feel good initially and will feel grieving or as if something has been stripped away - like someone walking by and snatching something out of your hands. When this happens you are appalled and shocked at first, but if it was something that was not for your good, you soon release your feelings and accept what has occurred. When God comes in a rending it is a supernatural act of judgment that immediately wipes away that which is not God while establishing His kingdom in its place. You may not readily know what to do with the experience and newness but these answers reside in you embracing and praising God for what He has done and absorbing the deliverance, healing and restoration that has taken place. As you come into this fellowship with God and His plan, He will begin to download how you are to operate in the new dimension of restoration that has not manifested.

God is all about reconciliation. Therefore, even as He would punish us for our sins, or allow us to reap the consequences of our actions, He is eager to rend. Even when it appears as if He has left us, He is right there waiting to reconcile. Waiting on us to call unto Him for deliverance and restoration.

> ***Isaiah 65:1*** *– I am sought of them that asked not for me; I am found of them that sought me not: I said, Behold me, behold me, unto a nation that was not called by my name. I have spread out my hands all the day unto a rebellious people, which walketh in a way that was not good, after their own thoughts;*
>
> ***The Amplified Version*** *- I WAS [ready to be] inquired of by those who asked not; I was [ready to be] found by those who sought Me not. I said,*

Here I am, here I am [says I AM] to a nation [Israel] that has not called on My name. I have spread out My hands all the day long to a rebellious people, who walk in a way that is not good, after their own thoughts;

The Message Version - *I've made myself available to those who haven't bothered to ask. I'm here, ready to be found by those who haven't bothered to look. I kept saying 'I'm here, I'm right here' to a nation that ignored me. I reached out day after day to a people who turned their backs on me, People who make wrong turns, who insist on doing things their own way.*

I believe this is what is happening in many regions and in world at large now:

Verse 2-7 The Message Version - *I reached out day after day to a people who turned their backs on me, People who make wrong turns, who insist on doing things their own way. They get on my nerves, are rude to my face day after day, Make up their own kitchen religion, a potluck religious stew.*

They spend the night in tombs to get messages from the dead, eat forbidden foods and drink a witch's brew of potions and charms. They say, 'Keep your distance. Don't touch me. I'm holier than thou.' These people gag me. I can't stand their stench. Look at this! Their sins are all written out—I have the list before me.

> *I'm not putting up with this any longer. I'll pay them the wages they have coming for their sins. And for the sins of their parents lumped in, a bonus.* "God says so. *"Because they've practiced their blasphemous worship, mocking me at their hillside shrines, I'll let loose the consequences and pay them in full for their actions."*

Matthew Henry Commentary states "*God looks at the heart, and vengeance is threatened for guilt.*" Even as God is angry in the scriptures above, as the people cry out (His remnant) for rending, He eagerly responds to the heart of the remnant through reconciliation rather than releasing further judgment upon the people and the land. Are you a part of a remnant that is to cry out for the region? The nation?

> **Verse 8-10 The Message Version** - *But just as one bad apple doesn't ruin the whole bushel, there are still plenty of good apples left. So I'll preserve those in Israel who obey me. I won't destroy the whole nation. I'll bring out my true children from Jacob and the heirs of my mountains from Judah.*
>
> *My chosen will inherit the land, my servants will move in. The lush valley of Sharon in the west will be a pasture for flocks, and in the east, the valley of Achor, a place for herds to graze. These will be for the people who bothered to reach out to me, who wanted me in their lives, who actually bothered to look for me.*

Rending is a quick work. When it is a season to rend and God's people call out for it, as quick as one repents, restoration begins. And as restoration occurs, God begin to release His blessings to His people.

> **Verse 17-25 The Message Version** - *Pay close attention now: I'm creating new heavens and a new earth. All the earlier troubles, chaos, and pain are things of the past, to be forgotten. Look ahead with joy. Anticipate what I'm creating: I'll create Jerusalem as sheer joy, create my people as pure delight. I'll take joy in Jerusalem, take delight in my people:*
> *No more sounds of weeping in the city, no cries of anguish; No more babies dying in the cradle, or old people who don't enjoy a full lifetime; One-hundredth birthdays will be considered normal–anything less will seem like a cheat.*
>
> *They'll build houses and move in. They'll plant fields and eat what they grow. No more building a house that some outsider takes over, No more planting fields that some enemy confiscates, for my people will be as long-lived as trees, my chosen ones will have satisfaction in their work. They won't work and have nothing come of it, they won't have children snatched out from under them. For they themselves are plantings blessed by God, with their children and grandchildren likewise God –blessed.*
>
> *Before they call out, I'll answer. Before they've finished speaking, I'll have heard. Wolf and lamb will graze the same meadow, lion and ox eat*

straw from the same trough, but snakes--they'll get a diet of dirt! Neither animal nor human will hurt or kill anywhere on my Holy Mountain," says God.

After the rending God begins to release His plan. Seek Him in all He desires for you personally and in your sphere. Also be obedient, and be generationally unmovable regarding what God speaks and requires of you. Obedience and an unmovable stance generationally sustains the work that was done in the rending.

Worship is a lifestyle of obedience:
Isaiah 66:1-3 The Message Version -
Heaven's my throne, earth is my footstool. What sort of house could you build for me? What holiday spot reserve for me? I made all this! I own all this!" God's Decree. "But there is something I'm looking for: a person simple and plain, reverently responsive to what I say.

The Amplified Version
THUS SAYS the Lord: Heaven is My throne, and the earth is My footstool. What kind of house would you build for Me? And what kind can be My resting-place? For all these things My hand has made, and so all these things have come into being [by and for Me], says the Lord. But this is the man to whom I will look and have regard: he who is humble and of a broken or wounded spirit, and who

trembles at My word and reveres My commands.

Be generationally unmovable in God:
Isaiah 66:22-23 The Message Version - For just as the new heavens and new earth that I am making will stand firm before me" -- God's Decree --"So will your children and your reputation stand firm. Month after month and week by week, everyone will come to worship me," God says.

The New English Translation Version - For just as the new heavens and the new earth I am about to make will remain standing before me," says the Lord, "So your descendants and your name will remain. From one month to the next and from one Sabbath to the next, all people b will come to worship me," says the Lord.

REFERENCES:

- *Article Like The Dew By Steven C. Wright*
- *The Christian Worldview Journal, Published Date: January 06, 2012*
- *Biblegateway.com*
- *Blueletterbible.com*
- *Crosswalk.com*
- *Merriam-Webster.com*
- *Dictionary.com*
- *Wikipedia.com*

Kingdom Shifters Books & Apparel
Available at Kingdomshifters.com

BOOKS FOR EVERYONE

Healing The Wounded Leader

Kingdom Shifters Decree That Thang

There Is An App For That

Kingdom Watchman Builder On the Wall

Embodiment Of A Kingdom Watchman Releasing The Vision

Dismantling Homosexuality Handbook Feasting In His Presence

Kingdom Heirs Decree That Thing

Let There Be Sight

Atmosphere Changers (Weaponry)

BOOKS FOR DANCERS

Dancers! Dancers! Decree That Thang

Spirits That Attack Dance Ministers & Ministries

TEE SHIRTS

Kingdom Shifters Tee Shirt

Let The Fruit Speak Tee Shirt

Releasing The Vision Tee Shirt

Kingdom Perspective Tee Shirt

Stand in Position Tee Shirt

No Defense Tee Shirt

My God Rules Like A Boss Tee Shirt

Destiny Blueprint Tee Shirt

CD'S

Decree That Thing CD

Kingdom Heirs Decree That Thing CD

Teachings & Worship CD's

www.ingramcontent.com/pod-product-compliance
Lightning Source LLC
LaVergne TN
LVHW051121080426
835510LV00018B/2165